Nine Titles

Also by Duncan Carmichael:

Official History of Ayr United Football Club Volume 1 – *Contour Press 1990.*
Official History of Ayr United Football Club Volume 2 – *Contour Press 1992.*
Images of Sport – Ayr United FC – *Tempus 2001.*
Ayr United Classics – *Tempus 2002.*
100 Ayr United Greats – *Tempus 2004.*
Walking Down the Somerset Road – *Fort Publishing 2006.*
Ayr United Miscellany – *Amberley Publishing 2011.*
Ayr United At War – *Mansion Field 2014.*
Ayr United On This Day – *Kennedy & Boyd 2016.*
Ayr United F.C. Managers - *Kennedy & Boyd 2017.*

Nine Titles
Ayr United triumphs

Duncan Carmichael

Kennedy & Boyd

Kennedy & Boyd
an imprint of
Zeticula Ltd
Unit 13
196 Rose Street
Edinburgh
EH2 4AT
Scotland

http://www.kennedyandboyd.co.uk
admin@kennedyandboyd.co.uk

First published in 2018

Copyright © Duncan Carmichael 2018
Cover design © Zeticula Ltd 2018

ISBN 978-1-84921-174-1
All rights reserved. No part of this publication may be reproduced, stored in a retrieval system, or transmitted in any form or by any means, electronic, mechanical, photocopying, recording or otherwise, without the prior permission of the publishers.

Acknowledgements

To David Sargent I am hugely indebted for the photograph of the players celebrating on the champions podium on 28th April, 2018. Many photographers captured this particular scene but David can be relied on to capture the Ayr United spirit better than anyone. He also kindly agreed to the use of a wonderfully evocative photograph taken by him at Alloa six days earlier.

Within these pages you will further see some programme illustrations with his work displayed on the front. With unfailing devotion he travels home and away, although being a resident of Innerleithen home games are that in name only.

Mark Kerr signed for Ayr United on Burns Day 2018 and in a true act of initiative the opportunity was seized to take him along to Burns Cottage. Graeme Miller I thank you for your enterprise and for permitting the use of your photograph of this scene.

"Everybody loves Lawrence Shankland" – these are the song words beloved of Ayr United supporters. After his wonderful season in 2017/18 he consented to renew his contract and Calum Campbell was there to capture the scene for posterity. Calum, I am indebted to you for your kind permission to use that image in this book. Ayr United supporters everywhere will doubtlessly agree that you and the rest of the team at Ayr United Media do a fantastic job in presenting first class coverage.

The *Ayrshire Post* and the *Ayr Advertiser* exist in a beautiful world of overwhelming Ayr United partisanship. There can be no greater praise. Throughout this book you will find quotes from both of these newspapers, quotes that display a passion for the club. Further gratitude is extended to the *Ayrshire Post* for the use of photographs from their archives.

It was necessary to check some information with the Scottish Football Museum. I thank Bruce Gilmour and Jim Thomson for their prompt co-operation.

The biggest acknowledgement of all goes to the Ayr United squad of 2017/18. That squad pulled off one of the nine title triumphs in the history of the club but these players merit special mention for providing the catalyst for this book.

Duncan Carmichael
Monkton, Ayrshire.
July 2018.

Contents

Introduction	ix
Second Division Champions 1911/12	1
Games and Players 1911/12	15
Second Division Champions 1912/13	21
Games and Players 1912/13	29
Second Division Champions 1927/28	35
Games and Players 1927/28	44
Second Division Champions 1936/37	51
Games and Players 1936/37	56
Second Division Champions 1958/59	63
Games and Players 1958/59	73
Second Division Champions 1965/66	83
Games and Players 1965/66	97
Second Division Champions 1987/88	105
Games and Players 1987/88	124
Second Division Champions 1996/97	137
Games and Players 1996/97	174
League One Champions 2017/18	189
Games and Players 2017/18	221
2017/18 – The Main Stats	231
Our League Titles – When and Where	232
A century in competitive matches	232
A century of goals in a season: the landmark scorers	233
Index	235

Illustrations

Ayr United FC 1911/12	2
One more to go — and yes, it was landed!	4
1911/12 beautifully summed up.	6
Ayr United versus Abercorn – the opening league game of 1911/12.	8
Ayr United at Dumbarton on 18th November 1911.	10
Ayr United versus St.Johnstone on 20th January, 1912.	12
Alex Hill Goodwin was always known as Hilly.	14
As a sprinter he represented Maryhill Harriers.	14
Sprigger White (far left) in later life.	18
Gerry McCrossan.	20
Ayr United FC 1912/13.	22
Ayr United versus Vale of Leven on 31st August, 1912.	24
Dumbarton versus Ayr United on 12th April, 1913.	26
David Thomson.	34
Ayr United FC 1927/28.	36
Ayr United players at Ayr seafront in the summer of 1928.	38
Tommy Kilpatrick, Danny Tolland and Jimmy Smith.	40
Ayr United FC 1936/37.	52
Davy Currie.	62
Ayr United FC in the summer of 1959.	64
Ayr United 6 Alloa Athletic 2.	66
By mid-November twelve league wins had been gained.	68
Ayr United 2 East Fife 0.	70
Fans felt let down because big wins were expected.	70
George McIntyre.	72
Bobby Thomson.	74
Jim McLean.	76
Jim McGhee.	78
Ayr United FC 1965/66.	84
The first home match of the league campaign resulted in defeat	86
Sam McMillan.	87
A late defeat but the fans were in good voice	89
Not what you would call a New Year derby!	90
January 1966 was hampered by 2-2 draws.	92

Super Sam in the Coronation Stakes	93
Stranraer 1 Ayr United 5.	94
Eddie Monan.	95
Second Division champions 1965/66.	96
Dick Malone.	98
Alex McAnespie.	100
Champions 1988	106
Programme cover: Ayr United v Arsenal	108
Programme cover: Ayr United v Reading.	110
Programme cover: Cowdenbeath v Ayr United.	112
Programme cover: Brechin City v Ayr United.	114
Programme cover: Albion Rovers v Ayr United.	116
Programme cover; Ayr United v East Stirling.	118
Ally MacLeod	121
Champions 1987/88 - Ian McAllister with the trophy.	122
Tommy Walker.	125
Henry Templeton.	127
Ian McAllister.	129
Kenny Wilson.	131
John Sludden.	133
10th May, 1997, at Berwick – Champions..	138
Programme cover: Ayr United v Hamilton Academical.	140
Alain Horace in action against Hamilton Accies..	141
Brechin City 1 Ayr United 1	143
John Traynor in action against Hamilton Accies..	145
Programme cover: Ayr United v Stenhousemuir.	146
Tom Smith unleashes a thunderbolt.	148
Stranraer 0 Ayr United 1.	149
Darren Henderson in the foreground.	150
Programme cover: Queen of the South v Ayr United.	152
Programme cover: Stenhousemuir v Ayr United.	154
Definitely not in Duncan George's collection!	156
John Traynor in action against Queen of the South.	158
Alain Horace has just scored against Dumbarton.	160
Paul Smith tangles with the Clyde defence.	161
Willie Jamieson after scoring against Berwick Rangers.	163
Mark Duthie in the colours of Ayr United.	164
Stevie Kerrigan (Paul Smith on right) after scoring.	166
Stevie Kerrigan in action against Queen of the South.	168

Program cover: Ayr United v Brechin City.	169
Paul Kinnaird takes on all comers.	171
Paul Smith (not in photo) has just scored.	172
David Castilla.	175
Isaac English, Kevin Biggart, Darren Henderson, Ronnie Coyle, John Traynor and Willie Jamieson	176
Robert Scott (right) with Jose Quitongo of Hamilton Accies and Mark Humphries (centre).	178
Jim Leishman (then manager of Livingston) and Gordon Dalziel.	180
Isaac English.	182
Ronnie Coyle	183
John Traynor	185
League One Winners 2017/18	190
Betfred Cup: Annan Athletic v Ayr United	192
Mark Kerr, here at Burns' Cottage.	194
Craig Moore (with the ball) has just scored at Alloa.	196
To the right are Alan Forrest and Craig McGuffie	196
Programme cover: Ayr United v. Stranraer.	198
Programme cover: Ayr United v Albion Rovers.	200
Programme cover: Ayr United v Queen's Park.	209
After his magnificent season Lawrence Shankland signed a new contract.	227

Introduction

In the world inhabited by devotees of Celtic and Rangers the concept of winning nine titles is familiar, the difference being that they glory in doing it consecutively then regaling it all in song. Such luxury is not afforded to the real fans who support provincial clubs.

Ayr United have succeeded in winning nine titles but this boast is tempered by admitting that this achievement has not been reached in the top tier and, even at that, it has taken since 1910. Fans can buy success at the price of a train ticket to Glasgow but Ayr United followers are made of sterner stuff. Title wins, by virtue of their relative rarity, are much more heavily appreciated.

Let's dip into the realms of fantasy and imagine that you are 120 years old and you have seen all of Ayr United's title wins right through from the first one in 1912 to the most recent in 2018. The question put to you is this: How many of these triumphs have triggered scenes of celebration at Somerset Park? The answer is one.

It is true that three titles have been clinched when the team has been playing at home but there was less capacity for instant communication in 1912 and 1928 and the crowd remained blissfully ignorant, for the time being, that the league had been won.

In 2018, by virtue of modern technology, the crowd had instant updates on the match elsewhere which was crucial to our fate. That 'elsewhere' was Kirkcaldy. With the final whistle already blown on the Ayr United versus Albion Rovers match, the fans and players silently waited on the Raith Rovers versus Alloa Athletic match finishing.

In those nervous minutes the only activity involved the frantic refreshing of score updates. Nervous minutes? Let's rephrase this and call them terror-stricken minutes!

In mentioning that three of the nine triumphs have occurred at Somerset Park, knowingly or not, it should not be assumed that six were clinched at away grounds. In 1913 and in 1959 it happened when the team was not even playing.

xiii

Hindsight can be a great comfort and that is partly the premise of this book. Knowing the outcome of a 'whodunnit' would be a spoiler. That notion will be turned on its head in the pages you are about to read. Far from being a spoiler it should be a source of satisfaction to know that each chapter will have a joyous climax.

Before proceeding please ponder on this. How many Scottish clubs can claim to have clinched a league title in England?

Second Division Champions

1911/12

Secretary-manager:
Harry Murray

Ayr United FC 1911/12

The only sound argument for amalgamating rival football clubs is one of financial prudence. It therefore begs the question of why such arrangements are not more prolific in a challenging economic climate. Even the suggestion of amalgamation is rare. To anyone with little or no interest in football this may seem an oddity. Yet the supposedly logical argument for mergers takes no cognisance of the passions entrenched within the followers of football clubs.

In 1910 the only ever amalgamation of two Scottish league clubs from the same town took place. This was the merger between Ayr FC and Parkhouse to create Ayr United. So are we to believe that harmony existed between these clubs? In truth there was a history of disharmony at club and fan level. The amalgamation went through in the mistaken belief that the new club would be voted straight into the First Division. The inaugural season ended in the attainment of a runners-up position in the Second Division.

This brings us to the topic of the club's first title win but, before proceeding, let's consider why the relationship between Ayr FC and Parkhouse was so fractured. It was largely attributable to the socio-economic factors. The Parkhouse club was based at Beresford Park which was conveniently located to the more prosperous areas south of the river. This enabled the club to attract a relatively well-heeled support. In contrast Ayr FC's Somerset Park base was convenient to the adjoining districts of Newton and Wallacetown at a time when large swathes of the housing remained barely fit for habitation.

The fiercest rivalry in world football today is that which exists between the Argentinian clubs Boca Juniors and River Plate. That hatred has its origin in the sensitive issue of social divides. It is self evident when you realise that the nickname of River Plate is Los Millonarios. The festering bitterness between Ayr FC and Parkhouse illustrated the same principle yet by August 1910 the poor and not so poor of Ayr mingled with each other in support of the new club.

An interesting side note is that the merger created a vacant place in the Second Division which was filled by Dundee Hibernian, founded one year earlier. That club was colloquially known as Dundee Hibs prior to the change of name to Dundee United in 1923.

In response to finishing as runners-up to Dumbarton in Ayr United's maiden season the *Ayrshire Post* opined: "There is no doubt that the method of automatic promotion in force in the English League competition is the right and proper one and should be adopted in Scotland."

One more to go — and yes, it was landed!

Adopting what was considered right and proper in Scottish football was an unlikely contingency in those years prior to the Great War. Then, as now, the most potent forces were greed and self interest. Automatic promotion would not occur until season 1921/22, pending which it was required to canvass support in the hope of being voted into the First Division.

The vagaries of the system meant that season 1911/12 got underway without Port Glasgow Athletic, voted out despite finishing above three other clubs. Voted into the vacant position was St.Johnstone. No clubs had managed to compile a compelling enough case for promotion. Under Bert Tickle's captaincy Ayr United proceeded to win the first nine league fixtures. This remains a club record league start. Within the time frame of that run seven matches were played in the Scottish Qualifying Cup. These were rounds one to five, including a first round replay, then a semi-final defeat at Dumbarton. The cup run succeeded in providing ample shooting practice. In the first three rounds Dumfries (5-1), Whithorn (10-0) and Thornhill (7-2) were slain at Somerset Park.

In the Whithorn match there was an incident which beautifully illustrated the one-sided nature of the tie. With the match still in progress goalkeeper Lee Massey and full-backs McKenzie and Gardiner took turns at posing for a photographer. This was in an age when photography was not an instant process. The crowd had a great laugh. Eccentricities are apt to occur when small clubs are involved. In that respect Thornhill did not disappoint. When the squad arrived at Ayr they had a goat for a mascot.

The club had decided to run a team at Junior level rather than a reserve side. Home matches were to be played at Beresford Park. Ayr United Juniors played their first match on 9th September, 1911. It was the occasion of a 1-0 defeat away to Craigmark Smithfield in the Ayr and District League. Participation at this level meant that Ayr United could field a team in the Scottish Junior Cup. Whereas this venture failed to bring any glory, Ayr United Juniors did win their first match in the competition when Carson Thistle were beaten 2-1 at home. Success in the Second Division ensured difficulty for aspiring understudies hoping to progress to first team level.

On 21st October, Dundee Hibs got slain 6-0 at Ayr with the consequence that Ayr United and Rangers were the only undefeated teams in the Scottish and English leagues. Switcher McLaughlan and Charlie Phillips scored coat-tricks that afternoon.

1911/12 beautifully summed up.

Coat-tricks? In the autumn of 1910 the club had struck its first commercial deal. The deal lasted for that autumn and the next three. The deal was done with Stewart's, a tailoring firm with a local branch at 224 High Street (two doors down from the Tam O'Shanter Inn on the Wallace Tower side). During the weeks of the offer an overcoat was to be awarded to any Ayr United player scoring two goals in a home league match, with a further overcoat going to a spectator nominated by the successful marksman. Four goals would see the prize doubled up.

Home form had been exceptional since the inception of the club. Abercorn had won 4-3 at Ayr on 26th November, 1910, and Ayr United's next home league defeat did not occur until 17th August, 1912, Abercorn again being the opposition. In those first two seasons of the club's existence no visiting club left Somerset Park with a clean sheet. Season 1911/12 continued to provide good value for the sixpenny admission cost. It was extra to enter the Stand. The 'Boys Gate', as it was termed, cost threepence. Ladies had the benefit of being admitted free. Particularly demonstrative in support of the team were the members of the Brake Club who congregated together at matches. In these formative years the colours were crimson and gold hooped shirts with blue shorts. Ayr United have completed five seasons unbeaten at home in the league. 1911/12 was the first of those.

Charlie Phillips, once of West Ham United, was a small player who lacked physique. In the gruelling world of olden-day football these attributes should have been major disadvantages, most especially for a centre-forward. Yet these flaws were negated by his craft, guile, speed and courage. He was destined to hit eighteen goals in this season's twenty-two league fixtures. For an away match against Leith Athletic on 25th November, he had a new partner at inside-forward. Making his debut was Jimmy Robertson, who had played for Chelsea in their inaugural season of 1905/06. Robertson was the scorer of Chelsea's second ever FA Cup goal and was now arriving at Ayr from Dundee Hibs.

On 16th December a league point was dropped for the first time in 1911 since 7th January. It happened in a 2-2 draw against Dundee Hibs at Tannadice Park. A week later a 4-2 home win over Leith Athletic left the club gloriously atop the table with this record.

Ayr United versus Abercorn – the opening league game of 1911/12.

	P	W	D	L	F	A	Points
Ayr United	11	10	1	0	34	11	21

The 'lost o' column had then to be revised after a 1-0 defeat at Perth on the last Saturday of the year. In those pre-Muirton Park years St.Johnstone played at the Recreation Ground. On this particular day the quagmire of a pitch got rolled before the match and the outcome was a surface which, according to the *Ayrshire Post* reporter, "shone like a glossy cookie". Jimmy Robertson was in the act of heading a certain goal when he got punched in the back and was almost knocked to the ground. No penalty!

In the 70th minute Bert Tickle conceded a penalty after supposedly fouling Brown. Tickle was an experienced player who had been at Preston North End as early as 1902. Here at Perth he was so frustrated at the penalty award that he asked Brown if he thought he had fouled him. The answer was 'no'. Loud protests abounded but McGowan paid no heed and calmly converted the award. Switcher McLaughlan had retired injured ten minutes earlier so a difficult struggle was rendered all the more difficult with the numerical disadvantage.

Two days later, on Monday 1st January, 1912, a crowd figure of 4,454 was recorded for the 3-2 home win over St.Bernard's. This number did not include ladies whom we were told were "well represented." The first three league fixtures of 1912 were won. Then the sequence was broken when St.Johnstone drew 1-1 at Ayr. Thus the first team to beat Ayr United in a league fixture in season 1911/12 also became the first opposition team in that campaign to depart Somerset Park with a league point. Then, after going to Barrhead and beating Arthurlie 1-0, the top of the table took on this aspect.

	P	W	D	L	F	A	Points
Ayr United	17	14	2	1	43	15	30
Abercorn	19	10	4	5	34	21	24
Dumbarton	17	11	1	5	34	22	23

With five games left the title could be guaranteed in one of two ways.

Option 1. Win the four-pointer at Dumbarton a week later.
Option 2. Take four points from the available ten.

Ayr United at Dumbarton on 18th November 1911 (Qualifying Cup semi-final).

Dumbarton 6 Ayr United 1. A Willie Black penalty put the team in the lead and it was 1-1 at half-time. In part the capitulation could have been excused by an injury crisis. Missing were Bert Tickle, Switcher McLaughlan, Hilly Goodwin and Harry Simpson. The next match should have been played at Meadow Park, Coatbridge. Albion Rovers, however, requested that the match should be switched to Ayr in anticipation of a better (shared) gate. Lack of support at home had been crippling their resources. In a very one-sided match Ayr United could afford the luxury of bad finishing and still win 4-0. On the same afternoon Dumbarton lost 4-2 to Dundee Hibs at Tannadice meaning that the title was won.

Our first and last titles have been won after beating Albion Rovers at Somerset Park but there were no scenes of elation in 1912 because there was not the same capacity for instant communication. It would have taken until the Saturday evening for the Dumbarton defeat to become apparent. That was when the paper boys would have been circulating the pubs to sell the football special. Temperance had strong support in the town at this time therefore those who had signed the pledge would not have known of the triumph until reading the Sunday papers.

The *Ayrshire Post* took particular pleasure in highlighting the wisdom of the amalgamation. "Lesson – A house divided against itself will not stand." There was one more target. Winning the last three games would give the club a Second Division record points total of thirty-eight. Hamilton Accies held the record with the thirty-seven points gained in season 1903/04. Alas the record stayed with that club, Ayr United taking just three points from those concluding matches.

In turn the team went on to beat Hurlford 2-0 in the Ayrshire Cup final and Annbank 2-0 in the Ayr Charity Cup final, both finals being staged at Beresford Park. Yet the event which would have the largest bearing on the season had yet to be staged. Would Ayr United be successful in the club's application to enter the First Division? Second Division runners-up in 1910/11 then champions in 1911/12 – that in itself should have been a cast iron case for inclusion. Financial stability, good transport links to Glasgow and the central belt, a superior playing surface, a 15,000-capacity ground, a 90,000 population within a fifteen-mile radius – the arguments touted in 1910 and 1911 got re-aired in 1912.

Ayr United versus St.Johnstone on 20th January, 1912.

Promotion hinged on the outcome of the annual general meeting of the Scottish Football League which was scheduled for the Monday evening of 3rd June. An extraordinary chain of events ensued. There was a motion from the Celtic delegate that the highest club in the Second Division should automatically pass into the First Division. The necessary two-thirds majority agreed. Then the St.Mirren delegate complained that the motion would mean the relegation of his club and he told the meeting that they had already committed themselves to a First Division wage bill.

In a mass show of gullibility it was decided to do a u-turn on the motion and that the matter of automatic promotion would be held over until the next annual general meeting. The *Ayrshire Post* concluded: "It was understood, however, that the meeting virtually decided for automatic promotion twelve months hence." The word 'virtually' implied doubt. In truth Scottish football remained a decade away from automatically promoting the Second Division's top club.

Alex Hill Goodwin was always known as Hilly.
As a sprinter he represented Maryhill Harriers.

Games and Players 1911/12

Game 1. 19th August, 1911, Somerset Park:
Ayr United 4 Abercorn 2.
Team: Massey, McKenzie, Gardiner, Dickson, Tickle, McLaughlan, A.H. Goodwin, Logan, Phillips, Simpson and Campbell.
Scorers: Archie Campbell, Charlie Phillips 2 and Bert Tickle.

Game 2. 26th August, 1911, North End Park:
Cowdenbeath 1 Ayr United 2.
Team: Massey, McKenzie, Gardiner, Dickson, Tickle, McLaughlan, A.H. Goodwin, Logan, Phillips, Simpson and Campbell.
Scorers: Charlie Phillips and Hugh Logan.

Game 3. 23rd September, 1911, Millburn Park:
Vale of Leven 2 Ayr United 3.
Team: Massey, McKenzie, Black, Connell, Tickle, McLaughlan, Dickson, Logan, Phillips, Simpson and Campbell.
Scorers: Switcher McLaughlan (penalty), Hugh Logan and Charlie Phillips.

Game 4. 7th October, 1911, Somerset Park:
Ayr United 2 East Stirling 0.
Team: Massey, Thomson, Black, Connell, Tickle, McLaughlan, A.H. Goodwin, Logan, Phillips, Simpson and Campbell.
Scorers: Hilly Goodwin and Archie Campbell.

Game 5. 21st October, 1911, Somerset Park:
Ayr United 6 Dundee Hibs 0.
Team: Massey, Thomson, Black, Connell, Tickle, McLaughlan, A.H. Goodwin, Logan, Phillips, Simpson and Campbell.
Scorers: Charlie Phillips 2, Hilly Goodwin, Switcher McLaughlan 2 (including a penalty) and Hugh Logan.

Game 6. 4th November, 1911, Somerset Park:
Ayr United 2 Albion Rovers 0.
Team: Massey, McKenzie, Black, Connell, Tickle, McLaughlan, A.H. Goodwin, Logan, Thomson, Simpson and Campbell.
Scorers: Bert Tickle and Switcher McLaughlan.

Abandoned after seventy-two minutes due to bad light. 11th November, 1911, Somerset Park:
Ayr United 1 Vale of Leven 1.
Team: Massey, Peddie, Black, Connell, Tickle, McLaughlan, A.H. Goodwin, Logan, Phillips, Simpson and Campbell.
Scorer: Charlie Phillips.
Vale of Leven arrived late due to a railway accident and the kick-off took place at 3.45 pm rather than 2.45 pm.

Game 7. 25th November, 1911, Logie Green:
Leith Athletic 1 Ayr United 3.
Team: Massey, Peddie, Black, Connell, Tickle, McLaughlan, A.H. Goodwin, Robertson, Phillips, Simpson and Campbell.
Scorers: Harry Simpson, Charlie Phillips and Archie Campbell.

Game 8. 2nd December, 1911, Somerset Park:
Ayr United 2 Dumbarton 1.
Team: Massey, Thomson, Black, Connell, Tickle, McLaughlan, A.H. Goodwin, Robertson, Phillips, Simpson and Campbell.
Scorers: Charlie Phillips and Hilly Goodwin.

Game 9. 9th December, 1911, Somerset Park:
Ayr United 4 Vale of Leven 0.
Team: Massey, Thomson, Black, Connell, Tickle, McLaughlan, A.H. Goodwin, Robertson, Phillips, Simpson and Campbell.
Scorers: Hilly Goodwin, Switcher McLaughlan (penalty) and Charlie Phillips 2.

Game 10. 16th December, 1911, Tannadice Park:
Dundee Hibs 2 Ayr United 2.
Team: Massey, Thomson, Black, Connell, Tickle, McLaughlan, A.H. Goodwin, Robertson, Phillips, Simpson and Campbell.
Scorers: Switcher McLaughlan (penalty) and Charlie Phillips.

Game 11. 23rd December, 1911, Somerset Park:
Ayr United 4 Leith Athletic 2.
Team: Massey, Thomson, Black, Connell, Tickle, McLaughlan, Logan, Robertson, Phillips, Simpson and Campbell.
Scorers: Switcher McLaughlan, Connell, Jimmy Robertson and Bert Tickle.

Game 12. 30th December, 1911, The Recreation Ground:
St.Johnstone 1 Ayr United 0.
Team: Massey, Thomson, Black, Connell, Tickle, McLaughlan, Logan, Robertson, Phillips, Simpson and Campbell.

Game 13. 1st January, 1912, Somerset Park:
Ayr United 3 St.Bernard's 2.
Team: Massey, Thomson, Black, Connell, Tickle, Fairlie, A.H. Goodwin, Robertson, Phillips, Simpson and Campbell.
Scorers: Harry Simpson, Bert Tickle (penalty) and Charlie Phillips.

Game 14. 6th January, 1912, Somerset Park:
Ayr United 3 Arthurlie 0.
Team: Massey, Thomson, Black, Connell, Tickle, Fairlie, A.H. Goodwin, Robertson, Phillips, Simpson and Campbell.
Scorers: Charlie Phillips 2 and Jimmy Robertson.

Game 15. 13th January, 1912, Ralston Park:
Abercorn 0 Ayr United 1.
Team: Massey, Thomson, Black, Connell, Tickle, Fairlie, A.H. Goodwin, Robertson, Phillips, Simpson and Campbell.
Scorer: Jimmy Robertson.

Game 16. 20th January, 1912, Somerset Park:
Ayr United 1 St.Johnstone 1.
Team: Gold, Black, Thomson, Connell, Mooney, McLaughlan, A.H. Goodwin, Robertson, Phillips, Simpson and Campbell.
Scorer: Switcher McLaughlan (penalty).

Game 17. 3rd February, 1912, Dunterlie Park:
Arthurlie 0 Ayr United 1.
Team: Massey, McKenzie, Black, Connell, Mooney, Fairlie, Campbell, Robertson, Phillips, Simpson and Dickson.
Scorer: Charlie Phillips.

Game 18. 10th February, 1912, Boghead Park:
Dumbarton 6 Ayr United 1.
Team: Massey, Black, Thomson, Connell, Mooney, Fairlie, Dickson, Robertson, Phillips, Logan and Campbell.
Scorer: Willie Black (penalty).

Sprigger White (far left) in later life.

Game 19. 17th February, 1912, Somerset Park (switched from Coatbridge):
Ayr United 4 Albion Rovers 0.
Team: Massey, Black, Thomson, Connell, Mooney, Fairlie, A.H. Goodwin, Robertson, Phillips, Simpson and Campbell.
Scorers: Hilly Goodwin, Harry Simpson 2 and Charlie Phillips.

Game 20. 16th March, 1912, Merchiston Park:
East Stirling 1 Ayr United 0.
Team: Massey, Black, Thomson, Connell, Mooney, McLaughlan, A.H. Goodwin, Robertson, Phillips, Simpson and Campbell.

Game 21. 30th March, 1912, The Gymnasium Ground:
St.Bernard's 2 Ayr United 2.
Team: Massey, Black, "Davidson", Connell, Mooney, McLaughlan, A.H. Goodwin, Robertson, Phillips, Simpson and Campbell.
Scorers: Jimmy Robertson and Charlie Phillips.

Game 22. 13th April, 1912, Somerset Park:
Ayr United 4 Cowdenbeath 0.
Team: Massey, Thomson, Hodge, Connell, Mooney, McLaughlan, A.H. Goodwin, Robertson, Phillips, Simpson and Campbell.
Scorers: Jimmy Robertson, Hilly Goodwin, Charlie Phillips and Archie Campbell.

Second Division top three 1911/12

	P	W	D	L	F	A	Points
Ayr United	22	16	3	3	54	24	35
Abercorn	22	13	4	5	43	22	30
Dumbarton	22	13	1	8	47	31	27

League goals

Charlie Phillips	18	Bert Tickle	4
Switcher McLaughlan	8	Hugh Logan	3
Hilly Goodwin	6	Willie Black	1
Jimmy Robertson	5	Wllie Connell	1
Archie Campbell	4	**Total**	**54**
Harry Simpson	4		

Gerry McCrossan.
He played for Ayr United in 1912/13 and went on to become a prominent educationalist who campaigned for the rights of teachers.

Second Division Champions

1912/13

Secretary-manager:
Harry Murray

Ayr United FC 1912/13.

Since the club had a championship flag to unfurl it was guaranteed that the bid to retain the title would begin at Somerset Park. On this occasion Abercorn came down from Paisley to supply opposition that was potentially daunting. In the previous campaign they had finished as runners-up and there was the chilling statistic that this club had inflicted Ayr United's last home league defeat back in November 1910. Considering the sense of occasion the crowd figure was moderate, although it did top 3,000. The mood was gradually deflated in a 2-0 defeat.

In time for the following week's fixture at Cowdenbeath an outstanding signing was made. The player was centre-half Sam Aitken who had played for Ayr FC on the historic occasion of Somerset Park's first ever Scottish League match back on 4th September, 1897 (Ayr FC 1 Linthouse 4). In May 1903 he was transferred to Middlesbrough. Here in 1912 he joined Ayr United from Raith Rovers.

A 1-1 draw at Cowdenbeath could have been defined as stabilising. In the next fixture a 6-0 home win over Vale of Leven might have been termed an annihilation. The opportunity for momentum was lost since the team toiled in the first round of the Scottish Qualifying Cup against Galston. Four consecutive matches were required to get through. Draws at Galston, Ayr and St.Mirren Park preceded an Ayr win at Rugby Park. Back to league business now? No! It was straight into round two and again it was not straightforward. It took a Somerset Park replay to get past Hurlford. At least Girvan Athletic were comfortably despatched (3-0 at home) in round three.

On winning 1-0 away to Albion Rovers on 19th October, seven weeks had elapsed since the last league fixture. One week hence it might even have been considered a mercy when the team exited the Scottish Qualifying Cup, beaten 2-1 away to Abercorn in cold, raw and windy conditions. On the same afternoon as the Abercorn tie Ayr United Juniors drew 2-2 with Mossblown Strollers in a Scottish Junior Cup tie played at Beresford Park.

The young Mossblown goalkeeper was signed by Ayr United on the strength of his performance. His name was Robert White, but he was better known as Sprigger and he immediately took over from Lee Massey. Sprigger was a sensation. In his first ten games for Ayr United (all league fixtures) he conceded just one goal and even that was from a penalty kick which he nearly saved. From 16th November, 1912, until 1st January, 1913, he had eight consecutive shutouts and this remains a

Ayr United versus Vale of Leven on 31st August, 1912.

club record. With all of these shutouts being in league fare he made a major contribution towards retaining the Second Division title. In the intervening years the closest threat to Sprigger's record has come from Davy Stewart who had six consecutive shutouts (five league, one Scottish Cup) between 28th December, 1968, and 1st February, 1969.

On the last day of November 1912, Willie McStay made his Ayr United debut at left-back. He came on loan from Celtic and remained until the summer of 1916. In time he would win the league four times with Celtic and the Scottish Cup three times but his first senior medal came with Ayr. McStay was aged just eighteen when making his first appearance in the crimson and gold but he demonstrated a maturity which belied his years. He remains Ayr United's youngest ever captain, being aged nineteen when being appointed to the role in August 1913. He was a great-uncle of Jock McStay who signed for Ayr United in 1996.

The other full-back at this stage of season 1912/13 was David Thomson who could boast Everton as a former club. Sam Aitken at centre-half had played at the top level with Middlesbrough and with a custodian of Sprigger White's calibre this Ayr team had a solid look. As already mentioned Charlie Phillips had played for West Ham United. You may also recall the mention of the frail build which did not deter him from scoring goals. As 1912/13 progressed his predatory instinct was still evident and he was on course for retaining his status of the club's top scorer.

However, the greatest Ayr United legend in this team was half-back Switcher McLaughlan. He had a cannonball shot and he still holds the record of scoring the most penalties for the club with twenty-seven.

January 1913 progressed with the team preserving the top spot. Then a winless run of three matches straddling January and February rendered it tenuous. Dundee Hibs versus Ayr United comprised bottom versus top yet in a match in which Charlie Phillips was heavily marked a 1-0 defeat was suffered. The crowd figure was so low that it yielded less than the £10 guarantee. Successive matches, both at home, produced 1-1 draws against Arthurlie and Dumbarton. Seven games were left and top place was still occupied but East Stirling had the same points total from the same number of games. Another lurking menace was Dunfermline Athletic who sat nine points behind but with six games in hand.

Dumbarton versus Ayr United on 12th April, 1913.

Yet the tension of it all required to be deferred pending the visit of Airdrie for a Scottish Cup tie. The crowd was estimated at 9,000 and the columns of the *Ayrshire Post* contained: "Enthusiasm in the district has never before been equalled in the history of the game." In losing 2-0 there was at least proof that the public had an appetite for matches against First Division clubs.

After three consecutive league wins the lead over East Stirling was stretched to four points but the danger still lay with Abercorn having games in hand. Consecutive defeats way to Johnstone and St.Bernard's then threatened to destroy the title aspirations. The Paisley area was well represented at league level by St.Mirren, Abercorn, Arthurlie and Johnstone but the pitch of the latter was shocking. Ironically the ground name was Newfield. The *Ayrshire Post* reporter said that it was "the worst pitch we have ever seen." He further reported: "In the last minutes Sam Aitken did not have a white spot on his face." It would not be the worst mud that he would endure in his life. The battlefields of the Somme ultimately left him almost blind.

On entering the season's final league fixture the only club that could beat Ayr United to the title was Abercorn. That finale was the occasion of a 1-0 loss at Dumbarton and to compound matters Abercorn won 1-0 at Cowdenbeath on the same day. Fortuitously Dumbarton replicated their form in midweek when our title rivals went down 3-0 at Boghead Park. To win the title Abercorn now required seven points from their five remaining games. A scoreless draw away to Albion Rovers then a 1-0 home defeat against Dunfermline Athletic left them requiring to win the last three matches. Abercorn 3 St.Bernard's 0 – it was now getting tense from an Ayr perspective. East Stirling 5 Abercorn 1 – Ayr United had now retained the title. Dunfermline Athletic 3 Abercorn 0 was of no importance.

Runners-up in 1910/11 and champions in seasons 1911/12 and 1913 – promotion now hinged on the yearly farce masquerading as the annual general meeting of the Scottish Football League. It took place on the Monday evening of 2nd June, 1913. Club chairman Tom Steen had worked hard in support of Ayr United's application.

He had to. The matter of league points was a lesser consideration than chamber eloquence. "Nothing has been talked about by football followers in Ayr since the close of last season but the United's prospects of promotion to the First League" – the *Daily Record* was commendably well informed. It was known that the result would be sent by telegram to the Ayrshire and Galloway Hotel, outside which a large crowd assembled in bad weather. There was great jubilation when the news came through that Ayr United had been promoted.

It had been proven that the Scottish Football League could display a reluctance to relegate clubs from the First Division. Had this body now relented? No they had not. There was no relegation in 1913. A decision had merely been made to extend the top tier by two clubs. The other promoted club was Dumbarton who had finished sixth, Yes, sixth! It was a ringing endorsement of a structure which had little cognisance of league points.

Games and Players 1912/13

Game 1. 17th August, 1912, Somerset Park:
Ayr United 0 Abercorn 2.
Team: Massey, Black, Thomson, Connell, Tickle, McLaughlan, H.J. Miles, Page, Phillips, Simpson and Campbell.

Game 2. 24th August, 1912, North End Park:
Cowdenbeath 1 Ayr United 1.
Team: Massey, Black, Thomson, Connell, Aitken, Tickle, Phillips, Peacock, Allan, Simpson and Campbell.
Scorer: Charlie Phillips.

Game 3. 31st August, 1912, Somerset Park:
Ayr United 6 Vale of Leven 0.
Team: Massey, Black, Thomson, Connell, Aitken, McLaughlan, Phillips, Peacock, Allan, Simpson and Campbell.
Scorers: Allan 2, Harry Simpson 3 and Peacock.

Game 4. 19th October, 1912, Meadow Park:
Albion Rovers 0 Ayr United 1.
Team: Massey, McCrossan, Thomson, Aitken, Connell, McLaughlan, Page, Simpson, Peacock, McGowan and Campbell.
Scorer: Harry Simpson.

Game 5. 2nd November, 1912, Somerset Park:
Ayr United 3 Albion Rovers 0.
Team: White, McCrossan, Thomson, Aitken, Tickle, McLaughlan, Allan, Simpson, Phillips, McGowan and Campbell.
Scorer: Charlie Phillips, Weir – own goal and Switcher McLaughlan.

Game 6. 9th November, 1912, Dunterlie Park:
Arthurlie 1 Ayr United 2.
Team: White, McCrossan, Thomson, Aitken, Connell, McLaughlan, Allan, Peacock, Simpson, McGowan and Campbell.
Scorers: Archie Campbell and Henry McGowan.

Game 7. 16th November, 1912, Somerset Park:
Ayr United 0 Dundee Hibs 0.
Team: White, McCrossan, Thomson, Aitken, Connell, McLaughlan, Allan, Peacock, Simpson, McGowan and Campbell.

Game 8. 23rd November, 1912, Somerset Park:
Ayr United 1 Cowdenbeath 0.
Team: White, McCrossan, Thomson, Aitken, Connell, McLaughlan, A.H. Goodwin, Simpson, Allan, McGowan and Campbell.
Scorer: Hilly Goodwin.

Game 9. 30th November, 1912, East End Park:
Dunfermline Athletic 0 Ayr United 0.
Team: White, McCrossan, McStay, Black, Aitken, McLaughlan, McKenna, Peacock, McGowan, Simpson and Campbell.

Game 10. 7th December, 1912, Somerset Park:
Ayr United 3 Leith Athletic 0.
Team: White, McCrossan, McStay, Black, Aitken, McLaughlan, Allan, Peacock, Newall, McGowan, and H. Thomson.
Scorers: Allan, Henry McGowan and Tom Newall.

Game 11. 14th December, 1912, Ralston Park:
Abercorn 0 Ayr United 0.
Team: White, D. Thomson, McStay, Aitken, Mooney, McLaughlan, Allan, Simpson, Newall, McGowan, and H. Thomson.

Game 12. 21st December, 1912, Merchiston Park:
East Stirling 0 Ayr United 0.
Team: White, Thomson, McStay, Aitken, Mooney, McLaughlan, Allan, Simpson, Peacock, McGowan, and Campbell.

Game 13. 28th December, 1912, Somerset Park:
Ayr United 5 Johnstone 0.
Team: White, Thomson, McStay, Aitken, Mooney, McLaughlan, Allan, Simpson, Phillips, McGowan, and Campbell.
Scorers: Henry McGowan 2 and Charlie Phillips 3.

Game 14. 1st January, 1913, Somerset Park:
Ayr United 3 St.Bernard's 0.
Team: White, Thomson, McStay, Aitken, Mooney, McLaughlan, Allan, Simpson, Phillips, McGowan, and A.H. Goodwin.
Scorers: Charlie Phillips 2 and Switcher McLaughlan.

Game 15. 4th January, 1913, The Recreation Ground:
St.Johnstone 3 Ayr United 3.
Team: White, Thomson, McStay, Aitken, Mooney, McLaughlan, A.H. Goodwin, Simpson, Phillips, McGowan and Campbell.
Scorers: Charlie Phillips, Switcher McLaughlan and Archie Campbell.

Game 16. 11th January, 1913, Somerset Park:
Ayr United 3 East Stirling 0.
Team: White, Thomson, McStay, Aitken, Mooney, McLaughlan, Allan, Simpson, Phillips, McGowan and A.H. Goodwin.
Scorers: Harry Simpson, Charlie Phillips and Switcher McLaughlan.

Game 17. 18th January, 1913, Tannadice Park:
Dundee Hibs 1 Ayr United 0.
Team: White, Thomson, McStay, Aitken, Mooney, McLaughlan, McKenna, Simpson, Phillips, McGowan and Campbell.

Game 18. 25th January, 1913, Somerset Park:
Ayr United 1 Arthurlie 1.
Team: White, Thomson, McStay, Aitken, Mooney, McLaughlan, Allan, Page, Phillips, McGowan and Campbell.
Scorer: Henry McGowan.

Game 19. 1st February, 1913, Somerset Park:
Ayr United 1 Dumbarton 1.
Team: Massey, Black, McStay, Aitken, Connell, McLaughlan, Allan, Simpson, Phillips, McGowan and Campbell.
Scorer: Archie Campbell.

Game 20. 22nd February, 1913, Logie Green:
Leith Athletic 1 Ayr United 4.
Team: White, Thomson, McStay, Aitken, Connell, McLaughlan, A.H. Goodwin, Phillips, Newall, McGowan and Campbell.
Scorers: Tom Newall 3 and Hilly Goodwin.

Game 21. 1st March, 1913, Millburn Park:
Vale of Leven 1 Ayr United 3.
Team: White, Thomson, McStay, Aitken, Connell, McLaughlan, A.H. Goodwin, Simpson, Newall, McGowan and Campbell.
Scorers: Hilly Goodwin, Switcher McLaughlan (penalty) and Tom Newall.

Game 22. 8th March, 1913, Somerset Park:
Ayr United 3 St.Johnstone 1.
Team: White, Thomson, McStay, Aitken, Connell, McLaughlan, A.H. Goodwin, Phillips, Newall, McGowan and Campbell.
Scorers: Switcher McLaughlan (penalty), Charlie Phillips and Sam Aitken.

Game 23. 15th March, 1913, Newfield:
Johnstone 2 Ayr United 1.
Team: White, Aitken, Thomson, Connell, Mooney, McLaughlan, A.H. Goodwin, Phillips, Newall, McGowan and Campbell.
Scorer: Henry McGowan.

Game 24. 22nd March, 1913, The Gymnasium Ground:
St.Bernard's 3 Ayr United 0.
Team: White, Thomson, McStay, Aitken, Connell, McLaughlan, A.H. Goodwin, Peacock, Phillips, McGowan and Campbell.

Game 25. 29th March, 1913, Somerset Park:
Ayr United 1 Dunfermline Athletic 0.
Team: White, Thomson, McStay, Aitken, Connell, McLaughlan, A.H. Goodwin, Phillips, Newall, McGowan and Campbell.
Scorer: Charlie Phillips.

Game 26. 12th April, 1913, Boghead Park:
Dumbarton 1 Ayr United 0.
Team: White, Thomson, McStay, Aitken, Connell, McLaughlan, A.H. Goodwin, Phillips, Newall, McGowan and Campbell.

Second Division top three 1912/13

	P	W	D	L	F	A	Points
Ayr United	26	13	8	5	45	19	34
Dunfermline	26	13	7	6	45	27	33
East Stirling	26	12	8	6	43	27	32

League goals

Charlie Phillips	11	Hilly Goodwin	3
Henry McGowan	6	Sam Aitken	1
Switcher McLaughlan	6	James Peacock	1
Tom Newall	5	Weir	
Harry Simpson	5	(Albion Rovers, own goal)	1
Willie Allan	3		
Archie Campbell	3	**Total**	**45**

David Thomson. Formerly of Everton he combined playing for Ayr United with his employment at the Ardeer Works. Despite the success of 1912/13 he became so disenchanted with football that he considered retiring from the game.

Second Division Champions

1927/28

Secretary-manager:
Archie Buchanan

Ayr United FC 1937/38

After being relegated on goal average in 1925 it was somewhat frustrating when two failed promotion attempts ensued. The frustration manifested itself in a meeting of supporters at the local Palais de Danse on the evening of 14th February, 1927. An *Ayr Advertiser* journalist informed readers that: "Dissatisfaction was expressed with the calibre of football in Ayr and it was agreed that steps should be taken to form a supporters' club." The consequence was a further meeting which packed out Ayr Town Hall on the evening of 3rd March. Provost Gould presided and a supporters' club was duly formed.

Yet the fans did not really need a representative voice to convey their feelings. The terracing fans and Standites at Somerset Park have always been able to convey the prevailing mood whether for better or worse. Here in 1927 they would soon be conveying it for the better – much better! At the time of its formation the Ayr United Supporters' Club wished to clarify that there was no wish to be antagonistic to the directors. The stated aims were encouragement and support. Time would prove that this was not just rhetoric. In the title-winning season ahead this organisation was so appreciative that, on two occasions, they gifted a ten-shilling note to each player as well as Alex Gillespie, the trainer.

1926/27 concluded with a 5-0 defeat at home to Dumbarton. This condemned the club to eighth place. There were few grounds for optimism that summer. For a pre-season trial match, which was open to public view, Jimmy Smith was given a game. In the previous season he had been playing for Rangers reserves in the Scottish Alliance having previously played for Dumbarton Harp and Clydebank. He scored five in that trial match. Coming events cast their shadows before – this old saying would prove to be emphatically true. Smith's sixty-six league goals in the season ahead would eventually put the name of Ayr United into the *Guinness Book of Records*.

A hat-trick in his first match – however, enthusiasm over Smith's feat was curbed by this league opener being no more than a 4-4 draw at home to St.Bernard's. By game four the club sat fifteenth in the twenty-club league having numbered a draw, a win and two defeats. Travelling to Barrhead and losing 4-1 to Arthurlie was put into context by that club losing 8-0 away to East Stirling the Saturday before. The fickleness of football was about to be illustrated. Starting the revival was a 5-3 home win over Albion Rovers in which Smith scored five in the first half. Within the columns of the *Ayr Advertiser* deserved

Ayr United players at Ayr seafront in the summer of 1928.

praise could be found: "A tireless worker and a first class opportunist, Smith, barring accidents, will score many goals for his new club."

Morton 0 Ayr United 2 – game ten put the club onto the summit of the league. The position was to remain unassailable. Bob Hepburn saved two penalties in this match and another conversational point was the manner of victory: "The ball was tapped from man to man with machine-like precision." That result at Cappielow Park was the fourth of seven consecutive league wins, the implication being that something went wrong when the sequence was broken. To be more precise a lot went wrong. Centre-half Felix McColgan could make nothing of Morrison, the Stenhousemuir centre-forward. The home team led 5-0 at half-time with Morrison netting four. McColgan was a good player on his day. It just so happened that this wasn't his day. He got released from his torment when being sent off in the second half. The final damage at Ochilview Park was 6-2. This brief slump was completed with a 2-0 defeat at Dumbarton a week later. The team then slipped neatly back into top gear. In the next thirteen league fixtures just one point was dropped. In the midst of that run there was a 6-1 home win over Arthurlie on the last day of 1927. The response to going behind in the second minute was a burst in which all of the Ayr goals were scored between the 28th and the 53rd minute. Goals four, five and six were scored within three minutes and the *Ayrshire Post* report hinted that this development allowed little time for the fans to draw breath: "These swiftly taken goals roused great enthusiasm amongst the spectators who cheered repeatedly." Smith got four in this match. By the season's end he was able to reflect on getting that total in three league matches in addition to twice hitting five. Six hat-tricks would also be included in his 66-goal haul.

It would be remiss to omit mention of the team mates who helped to supply the chances so clinically converted. Inside-right Danny Tolland was hugely popular with the fans for his supreme skill. Quite simply, he was a natural footballer, who was a delight to watch. Before Smith's arrival he had been experimented with at centre-forward but he was better suited to the type of position that, in the main, would allow him to create chances. In the dressing room he was equally popular due to his extrovert nature and sharp wit. At inside-left was Billy Brae, who was able to display intricate skill if required but he was more apt to be direct. His twelve-year Ayr United career span (1923 – 1935) was a club record at the time and he remains one of just five

Left to right: Tommy Kilpatrick, Danny Tolland and Jimmy Smith.

players to have scored more than one hundred league goals for the club. There was a run of five consecutive seasons in which he was the second top scorer. On the right wing was Jim Nisbet who was destined to become a Scotland player while still attached to Ayr United and the same was true of goalkeeper Bob Hepburn. The half-back line was combative. Since it contained a player known as Warhorse Wullie Robertson it could have been no other way. Robertson went on to play for Stoke City and Manchester United. In analysing the strength of this Ayr United team it would be tempting to suggest that it had a balanced look. Yes, it was strong in the key areas barring the odd lapse but it was a team primed to attack. Willie Fleming was the captain. He played mainly at left-back and occasionally at centre-half, yet this was a player who was fielded at centre-forward when signed from Celtic in August 1925 and who scored a hat-trick on his Ayr United debut.

Eliminating Bo'ness from the Scottish Cup with a 2-0 home win was a giantkilling act in the loosest sense since the victorious team was rampant in the Second Division while the vanquished team was struggling unsuccessfully to stave off relegation in the First Division. The visit of Falkirk in the second round stood to be a more accurate measure of what Ayr United would face in the almost certain event of promotion. That tie was lost 4-2 to put the focus solely on the league.

On the last Saturday in February, Jimmy Smith bagged four goals in a 7-3 destruction at home to Arbroath. Eight fixtures now remained and the top of the table took on an aspect which even the most bitter of pessimists could not have found fault with. Two of the five defeats had happened inside the first four matches and they were now a distant memory.

	P	W	D	L	F	A	Points
Ayr United	30	22	3	5	99	45	47
Dundee United	30	15	7	8	69	51	37

At two points for a win there was little danger and the already buoyant morale was boosted further with Jimmy Smith's assurance that he would definitely be remaining at the club for season 1928/29.

The title was clinched with five games to spare, albeit that the occasion was rendered slightly inauspicious by it happening on the day of a 1-0 defeat at home to Dumbarton, who had entered the match as the second bottom club. It was odd too that Ayr United took no points off low-placed Dumbarton in a generally dominant season. Dundee United losing at home to East Fife created the mathematical certainty of the status of champions. It being 1928 the fans would have drifted from the ground, completely oblivious of the result at Tannadice. The Dumbarton match was the third of four fixtures which yielded two draws and two defeats.

Jimmy Smith was now chasing the British goal scoring record set by George Camsell of Middlesbrough in the previous season. Camsell's total was fifty-nine league goals. With four games left Smith was on fifty-seven. For the visit of East Stirling it was a reachable target. East Stirling taking the lead in the second minute was not in the script. A penalty to Ayr provided a gilt edged opportunity for both the equaliser and goal fifty-eight. Smith missed it! He atoned by scoring a great equaliser four minutes before half-time. Camsell's record was equalled in the 60th minute. According to the *Ayr Advertiser* it was "a doubtful goal since he seemed well offside." The *Ayrshire Post* agreed that he was in an offside position but considered it a legitimate goal because the ball touched a defender on its way through to him. For the remainder of the match he was constantly plied with the ball but he was heavily marked.

The action now moved to Cathkin Park for a Monday afternoon fixture. In the midst of a 3-3 draw with Third Lanark, Smith hit goal number sixty with a left-foot shot twelve minutes into the second half. This was, at the time, the record breaking goal but it was not anticipated that Dixie Dean would net sixty league goals for Everton in the season still in progress. In retrospect we can now see that he needed one more. Goal sixty-one came later in the match. Four more in a 7-1 rout at home to Dundee United and the consolation goal in a 2-1 defeat away to Leith Athletic took it to sixty-six league goals for the season and 117 for the team.

On the Friday evening of 18th May the Cattle Market Inn hosted a celebratory dinner at which club director Lawrence Gemson presented Smith with a wallet of notes. Mr Gemson had a special mention for team captain Willie Fleming and Ben Popplewell. Ben Popplewell? Throughout the season the Ayr United players were his guests at the Gaiety Theatre every Friday evening.

On the morning after the event at the Cattle Market Inn the squad departed Ayr by the 9 am train for Glasgow. A further train was taken to Newcastle, the place of embarkation for a gruelling voyage to Oslo. The tour comprised three wins and a defeat against teams from Norway and a spectacular 3-1 victory over the Swedish national team in Stockholm. Jimmy Smith scored ten on the tour, including two against Sweden.

Games and Players 1927/28

Game 1. 13th August, 1927, Somerset Park:
Ayr United 4 St.Bernard's 4.
Team: Hepburn, Woodburn, Dean, Robertson, Fleming, Melville, Nisbet, Tolland, Smith, McCosh and Walters.
Scorers: Jimmy Smith 3 and Jim Nisbet.

Game 2. 20th August, 1927, Forthbank:
King's Park 2 Ayr United 1.
Team: Hepburn, Purdon, Dean, Robertson, Fleming, Melville, Nisbet, Tolland, Smith, McCosh and Walters.
Scorer: Jim Nisbet.

Game 3. 27th August, 1927, Somerset Park:
Ayr United 3 Alloa Athletic 0.
Team: Hepburn, Purdon, Dean, Robertson, Fleming, Turnbull, Nisbet, Tolland, Smith, Brae and Kilpatrick.
Scorers: Jimmy Smith 2 and Billy Brae.

Game 4. 3rd September, 1927, Dunterlie Park:
Arthurlie 4 Ayr United 1.
Team: Hepburn, Purdon, Dean, Robertson, Fleming, Turnbull, Nisbet, McColgan, Smith, Brae and Kilpatrick.
Scorer: Billy Brae.

Game 5. 10th September, 1927, Somerset Park:
Ayr United 5 Albion Rovers 3.
Team: Hepburn, Purdon, Fleming, Robertson, McColgan, Turnbull, Nisbet, Tolland, Smith, Brae and Kilpatrick.
Scorer: Jimmy Smith 5.

Game 6. 17th September, 1927, Mill Park:
Bathgate 1 Ayr United 1.
Team: Hepburn, Purdon, Fleming, Robertson, McColgan, Turnbull, Nisbet, Tolland, Smith, Brae and Kilpatrick.
Scorer: Danny Tolland.

Game 7. 24th September, 1927, Somerset Park:
Ayr United 7 Forfar Athletic 0.
Team: Hepburn, Purdon, Fleming, Robertson, McColgan, Turnbull, Nisbet, Tolland, Smith, Brae and Kilpatrick.
Scorers: Jim Nisbet 3, Jimmy Smith 3 (including a penalty) and Billy Brae.

Game 8. 1st October, 1927, Clydeholm Park:
Clydebank 1 Ayr United 4.
Team: Hepburn, Purdon, Fleming, Robertson, McColgan, Turnbull, Nisbet, Tolland, Smith, Brae and Kilpatrick.
Scorers: Jimmy Smith 3 and Billy Brae.

Game 9. 8th October, 1927, Somerset Park:
Ayr United 3 Queen of the South 1.
Team: Hepburn, Purdon, Fleming, Robertson, McColgan, Turnbull, Nisbet, Tolland, Smith, Brae and Kilpatrick.
Scorers: Danny Tolland, Jim Nisbet and Billy Brae.

Game 10. 15th October, 1927, Cappielow Park:
Morton 0 Ayr United 2.
Team: Hepburn, Purdon, Fleming, Robertson, McColgan, Turnbull, Nisbet, Tolland, Smith, Brae and Kilpatrick.
Scorer: Billy Brae 2.

Game 11. 22nd October, 1927, Gayfield Park:
Arbroath 0 Ayr United 2.
Team: Hepburn, Purdon, Fleming, Robertson, McColgan, Turnbull, Nisbet, Tolland, Smith, Brae and Kilpatrick.
Scorers: Jimmy Smith and Danny Tolland.

Game 12. 29th October, 1927, Somerset Park:
Ayr United 3 East Fife 0.
Team: Hepburn, Purdon, Fleming, Robertson, McColgan, Turnbull, Nisbet, Tolland, Smith, Brae and Kilpatrick.
Scorers: Jimmy Smith, Billy Brae and Jim Nisbet.

Game 13. 5th November, 1927, Somerset Park:
Ayr United 6 Third Lanark 2.
Team: Hepburn, Purdon, Fleming, Robertson, McColgan, Turnbull, Nisbet, Tolland, Smith, Brae and Kilpatrick.
Scorers: Jim Nisbet, Billy Brae 2, Tommy Kilpatrick and Jimmy Smith 2.

Game 14. 12th November, 1927, Ochilview Park:
Stenhousemuir 6 Ayr United 2.
Team: Hepburn, Purdon, Fleming, Robertson, McColgan, Turnbull, Nisbet, Tolland, Smith, Brae and Kilpatrick.
Scorer: Billy Brae 2.

Game 15. 19th November, 1927, Boghead Park:
Dumbarton 2 Ayr United 0.
Team: Hepburn, Purdon, Fleming, Robertson, Watson, Turnbull, Nisbet, Tolland, Smith, Brae and Kilpatrick.

Game 16. 26th November, 1927, Somerset Park:
Ayr United 5 Armadale 0.
Team: Hepburn, Purdon, Fleming, Robertson, Watson, Turnbull, Nisbet, Simpson, Smith, Brae and Kilpatrick.
Scorers: Jimmy Smith 3 (including a penalty), Billy Brae and Jim Nisbet.

Game 17. 3rd December, 1927, Firs Park:
East Stirling 2 Ayr United 3.
Team: Hepburn, Purdon, Fleming, Robertson, McColgan, Turnbull, Nisbet, Simpson, Smith, Brae and Kilpatrick.
Scorer: Jimmy Smith 3.

Game 18. 10th December, 1927, Tannadice Park:
Dundee United 1 Ayr United 3.
Team: Hepburn, Purdon, Fleming, Robertson, McColgan, Turnbull, Nisbet, Simpson, Smith, Brae and Kilpatrick.
Scorers: Billy Brae, Jimmy Smith and Tommy Kilpatrick.

Game 19. 17th December, 1927, Somerset Park:
Ayr United 3 Leith Athletic 1.
Team: Hepburn, Purdon, Fleming, Robertson, McColgan, Turnbull, Nisbet, McCosh, Smith, Simpson and Kilpatrick.
Scorers: Jocky Simpson and Jimmy Smith 2 (including a penalty).

Game 20. 24th December, 1927, The Gymnasium Ground:
St.Bernard's 0 Ayr United 4.
Team: Hepburn, Purdon, Fleming, Robertson, McColgan, Turnbull, Nisbet, Tolland, Smith, Simpson and Kilpatrick.
Scorers: Jocky Simpson, Jimmy Smith 2 and Tommy Kilpatrick.

Game 21. 31st December, 1927, Somerset Park:
Ayr United 6 Arthurlie 1.
Team: Hepburn, Purdon, Fleming, Robertson, McColgan, Turnbull, Nisbet, Tolland, Smith, Simpson and Kilpatrick.
Scorers: Jimmy Smith 4, Jim Nisbet and Danny Tolland.

Game 22. 2nd January, 1928, Somerset Park:
Ayr United 4 Morton 1.
Team: Hepburn, Purdon, Fleming, Robertson, McColgan, Turnbull, Nisbet, Tolland, Smith, Simpson and Kilpatrick.
Scorers: Willie Robertson, Jimmy Smith 2 and Danny Tolland.

Game 23. 3rd January, 1928, Cliftonhill Park:
Albion Rovers 1 Ayr United 1.
Team: Hepburn, Purdon, Fleming, Robertson, McColgan, McCall, Nisbet, Tolland, Smith, Brae and Kilpatrick.
Scorer: Billy Brae.

Game 24. 7th January, 1928, Recreation Park:
Alloa Athletic 1 Ayr United 3.
Team: Hepburn, Purdon, Fleming, Robertson, McColgan, Turnbull, Nisbet, Tolland, Smith, Brae and Kilpatrick.
Scorer: Jimmy Smith 3.

Game 25. 14th January, 1928, Somerset Park:
Ayr United 7 Bathgate 2.
Team: Hepburn, Purdon, Fleming, Robertson, McColgan, Turnbull, Nisbet, Tolland, Smith, Brae and Kilpatrick.
Scorers: Billy Brae 2 and Jimmy Smith 5 (including a penalty).

Game 26. 28th January, 1928, Palmerston Park:
Queen of the South 2 Ayr United 4.
Team: Hepburn, Purdon, Fleming, Robertson, McColgan, Turnbull, Nisbet, Tolland, Smith, Brae and Kilpatrick.
Scorers: Jimmy Smith 2, Billy Brae and Jim Nisbet.

Game 27. 8th February, 1928, Somerset Park:
Ayr United 3 Clydebank 1.
Team: Hepburn, Purdon, Fleming, Robertson, McColgan, Turnbull, Nisbet, Tolland, Smith, Brae and Kilpatrick.
Scorers: Jim Nisbet, Jimmy Smith and Felix McColgan.

Game 28. 11th February, 1928, Station Park:
Forfar Athletic 1 Ayr United 2.
Team: Hepburn, Purdon, Fleming, Robertson, McColgan, Turnbull, Nisbet, Tolland, Smith, Brae and Kilpatrick.
Scorers: Jim Nisbet and Jimmy Smith.

Game 29. 18th February, 1928, Bayview Park:
East Fife 2 Ayr United 0.
Team: Hepburn, Purdon, Fleming, Robertson, McColgan, Turnbull, Nisbet, Tolland, Smith, Brae and Kilpatrick.

Game 30. 25th February, 1928, Somerset Park:
Ayr United 7 Arbroath 3.
Team: Hepburn, Purdon, Fleming, Robertson, Watson, Turnbull, Nisbet, Tolland, Smith, Brae and "Jackson".
Scorers: Jimmy Smith 4, Billy Brae and Danny Tolland 2.

Game 31. 3rd March, 1928, Somerset Park:
Ayr United 2 King's Park 2.
Team: Hepburn, Purdon, Fleming, Robertson, Watson, Turnbull, Kilpatrick, Tolland, Smith, Brae and Inglis.
Scorer: Jimmy Smith 2 (including a penalty).

Game 32. 17th March, 1928, Somerset Park:
Ayr United 2 Stenhousemuir 2.
Team: Hepburn, Purdon, Fleming, Robertson, Watson, Turnbull, Nisbet, Tolland, Smith, Brae and Kilpatrick.
Scorers: Jimmy Smith and Danny Tolland.

Game 33. 24th March, 1928, Somerset Park:
Ayr United 0 Dumbarton 1.
Team: Hepburn, Price, Fleming, Robertson, McColgan, McCall, Nisbet, Simpson, Smith, Brae and Kilpatrick.

Game 34. 31st March, 1928, Volunteer Park:
Armadale 3 Ayr United 1.
Team: Hepburn, Price, Fleming, Robertson, McColgan, McCall, Nisbet, Tolland, Smith, Brae and Kilpatrick.
Scorer: Jimmy Smith.

Game 35. 7th April, 1928, Somerset Park:
Ayr United 2 East Stirling 1.
Team: Hepburn, Purdon, Dean, Robertson, Watson, McCall, Nisbet, Tolland, Smith, Brae and Kilpatrick.
Scorer: Jimmy Smith 2.

Game 36. 9th April, 1928, Cathkin Park:
Third Lanark 3 Ayr United 3.
Team: Hepburn, Purdon, Fleming, Robertson, McColgan, Turnbull, Nisbet, Tolland, Smith, Simpson and Brae.
Scorers: Billy Brae and Jimmy Smith 2.

Game 37. 14th April, 1928, Somerset Park:
Ayr United 7 Dundee United 1.
Team: Hepburn, Purdon, Fleming, Robertson, McColgan, Turnbull, Nisbet, Tolland, Smith, Simpson and Brae.
Scorers: Danny Tolland, Jimmy Smith 4 (including a penalty), Jocky Simpson and Billy Brae.

Game 38. 21st April, 1928, Powderhall:
Leith Athletic 2 Ayr United 1.
Team: Hepburn, Purdon, Fleming, Robertson, McColgan, Turnbull, Nisbet, Tolland, Smith, "Cameron" and Brae.
Scorer: Jimmy Smith.

Second Division top three 1927/28

	P	W	D	L	F	A	Points
Ayr United	38	24	6	8	117	60	54
Third Lanark	38	18	9	11	100	66	45
King's Park	38	16	12	10	74	68	44

League goals

Jimmy Smith	66	Jocky Simpson		3
Billy Brae	21	Felix McColgan		1
Jim Nisbet	13	Willie Robertson		1
Danny Tolland	9	**Total**		**117**
Tommy Kilpatrick	3			

Second Division Champions

1936/37

Manager:
Frank Thompson

Ayr United FC 1936/37.

The three title wins to this point of history had been gained without a manager in the conventional sense. In 1911/12 and 1912/13 the nearest the club had to a manager was Harry Murray, but his duties were entirely administrative. Even if his experience had been in football rather than clerical he would not have had an exclusive say in team selection anyway. The protocol of the time meant that the board selected the team, although his presence in the boardroom would have allowed him at least the opportunity for input. Tactics were dictated by the more experienced players, or those players of a more talkative nature.

When the team triumphed in 1927/28 the manager was Archie Buchanan, whom your writer once had the privilege of interviewing. Despite having the word 'manager' in his job title Mr Buchanan's duties bore comparison to those of his predecessor Mr Murray. There was no responsibility for recruiting players and he had positively no say in tactics. Again though he was present in the boardroom when team selection was under discussion.

Season 1936/37 was to see the club's first league title under the guidance of a man with a proper background in football. In his day Frank Thompson was an outside-left who won the Irish Cup with Cliftonville in 1909 and the FA Cup with Bradford City in 1911. He could also reflect on twelve international appearances for Ireland. When he occupied the manager's chair at Somerset Park there was still a heavy requirement to fulfil clerical duties but he could pass the 'show us your medals' test.

This would be the season in which the team would amass 122 league goals and this remains a club record. So who scored the first one? Please do not trouble yourself by trying to conjure up names of club legends who played at this time. It was scored by Richardson, the Leith Athletic right-back, who obligingly headed the ball past his own goalkeeper for an own goal. That was an equaliser and Bud Fisher went on to head the winner but the *Ayr Advertiser* rightly claimed that the manner of beating Leith Athletic 2-1 at home had been unconvincing.

A fortnight later another Edinburgh club departed Ayr with an odd-goal defeat and the *Ayr Advertiser* again described it as unconvincing. In reporting on a 3-2 win over Edinburgh City the reporter used the expression "scraped through." On the Saturday between those fixtures a 3-2 win at Montrose concluded with the home team battling for an equaliser. Maximum points were taken from the opening three games yet there were no convincing performances. It could be argued that this is the hallmark of champions. Losing 2-0 away to East Stirling in fixture four simply destroyed that argument.

On the first Saturday in October, East Fife were beaten 4-1 at Ayr and the *Ayr Advertiser* reporter replenished his stock of mood descriptions by telling his readers that "people are still grumbling." It eased the club into third place but the public had still to be convinced. Frank Thompson then made a bold foray into the transfer market. He signed Eddie Summers, Albert Smith and Jock Mayes. All were acquired from Clyde and Mr Thompson had signed all three for that club when he was the manager there.

The impact was not immediate but it was close to it. A 1-1 draw at Airdrie preceded twelve consecutive league wins and this remains a club record. The nearest threat to that record came in 1968/69 when Ally MacLeod's team mustered eleven consecutive league wins.

Terry McGibbons remains Ayr United's all-time second-highest scorer of league goals and he struck form with a vengeance during that invincible run spanning 24th October, 1936, until 2nd January, 1937.

Brechin City, Stenhousemuir and Montrose bore the brunt with each conceding eight goals at Ayr. These twelve games produced sixty-four goals for Ayr United. Let us just reconsider that statistic. Over the course of twelve consecutive league games the team averaged five per match and there were four goals to spare. You are sure to understand that the magnitude of it all is deserving of re-emphasis.

When the run came to an end Frank Thompson was absent. He was in Glasgow to indulge in some talent spotting. The sequence finished at Meadowbank, the ground of Leith Athletic. Terry McGibbons and John Torbet had the team 2-0 ahead by the ninth minute. Then, according to the *Ayr Advertiser*, "Ayr United treated the crowd to fancy football." The home team felt disinclined towards standing back and admiring this so-called fancy football and the match was lost 3-2. John Torbet's 86th minute penalty miss put the seal on a match squandered through complacency.

A harsh lesson was learned and the winning habit was resumed.

With seven games left the top of the Second Division looked like this.

	P	W	D	L	F	A	Points
Ayr United	27	21	2	4	99	37	44
St.Bernard's	26	17	4	5	79	37	38

The next match was rendered all the more interesting since it was a clash of the top two at Ayr. Further intriguing was the prospect of the 100th goal. In going 2-0 down in the 29th minute it was considered that the anxiety of the spectators was adversely affecting the players. Five minutes afterwards Hyam Dimmer got the landmark strike with the back of his head. After the interval there were no signs of anxiety. Four goals in the last half hour created a 5-2 victory which made the chance of winning the title a virtual certainty, and it was barely mid-February.

For the visit of Morton on 20th March the crowd topped 12,000. It was a vital game for the visitors since they sat one point behind second-placed St.Bernard's with a game in hand therefore the second promotion place was viable for them. It finished 1-1 and by the season's conclusion this would be the club's only point dropped at home in the entire season. Frank Thompson was not there. He had been in a Prestwick Nursing Home for three weeks prior to this match. Although discharged on the day before, he was confined to his bed at home.

One week later the result Ayr United 5 King's Park 0 guaranteed promotion but not the title. The club record for league goals in a season was the 117 scored in 1927/28. When the final whistle blew the total was 119. It was the last home fixture and to date it had been a wonderful one for those supporters who had been justifiably unconvinced in the opening weeks.

During strong periods in the club's history the expression 'Fortress Somerset' has been used in relation to the sense of foreboding experienced by rival clubs playing at Ayr. With thirty-three out of a possible thirty-four home points that expression had special resonance for season 1936/37.

Raith Rovers 2 Ayr United 2 – after coming from 2-0 down the title winning point was gained. A 4-1 loss away to East Fife on a Friday night was an inconsequential finale. When Bob Smith went off injured, right-back Eddie Summers had to complete the game in goal. Again it was a minor consideration. The season's work had already been done most satisfactorily.

Games and Players 1936/37

Game 1. 8th August, 1936, Somerset Park:
Ayr United 2 Leith Athletic 1.
Team: Watson, Bourhill, Strain, Clancy, Currie, Hernon, Fisher, McGibbons, McNeill, Dimmer and Torbet.
Scorers: Richardson – own goal and Bud Fisher.

Game 2. 15th August, 1936, Links Park:
Montrose 2 Ayr United 3.
Team: Smith, Bourhill, Strain, Clancy, Currie, Steele, Fisher, McGibbons, McNeill, Dimmer and Torbet.
Scorers: Hyam Dimmer 2 and John Torbet.

Game 3. 22nd August, 1936, Somerset Park:
Ayr United 3 Edinburgh City 2.
Team: Smith, Bourhill, Strain, Clancy, Currie, Hernon, Fisher, Dimmer, McGibbons, Steele and Torbet.
Scorers: Terry McGibbons 2 and Hyam Dimmer.

Game 4. 29th August, 1936, Firs Park:
East Stirling 2 Ayr United 0
Team: Smith, Dyer, Strain, Clancy, Currie, Bourhill, Fisher, Dimmer, McGibbons, Gemmell and Torbet.

Game 5. 5th September, 1936, Somerset Park:
Ayr United 6 Forfar Athletic 1.
Team: Smith, Dyer, Strain, Clancy, Currie, Taylor, Fisher, Dimmer, McGibbons, Gemmell and Torbet.
Scorers: Terry McGibbons 2, Hyam Dimmer, David Gemmell 2 and Bud Fisher.

Game 6. 12th September, 1936, Central Park:
Cowdenbeath 2 Ayr United 1.
Team: Smith, Bourhill, Strain, Clancy, Currie, Steele, Fisher, Dimmer, McGibbons, Gemmell and Torbet.
Scorer: Terry McGibbons.

Game 7. 19th September, 1936, Somerset Park:
Ayr United 4 Dundee United 1.
Team: Smith, Bourhill, Strain, Clancy, Currie, Kenmuir, Gibson, Dimmer, McGibbons, Gemmell and Torbet.
Scorers: Terry McGibbons 2, Hyam Dimmer and John Torbet.

Game 8. 26th September, 1936, Ochilview Park:
Stenhousemuir 1 Ayr United 1.
Team: Smith, Bourhill, Strain, Taylor, Currie, Steele, Gibson, Dimmer, McGibbons, Gemmell and Torbet.
Scorer: William Gibson.

Game 9. 3rd October, 1936, Somerset Park:
Ayr United 4 East Fife 1.
Team: Smith, Bourhill, Strain, Clancy, Currie, Taylor, Black, Dimmer, McGibbons, Gemmell and Torbet.
Scorers: John Torbet, Terry McGibbons, Jock Taylor and Hyam Dimmer.

Game 10. 10th October, 1936, Cappielow Park:
Morton 3 Ayr United 2.
Team: Smith, Bourhill, Strain, Clancy, Currie, Taylor, Steele, Dimmer, McGibbons, Gemmell and Torbet.
Scorers: Hyam Dimmer and David Strain (penalty).

Game 11. 17th October, 1936, Broomfield Park:
Airdrie 1 Ayr United 1.
Team: Bob Smith, Bourhill, Strain, Clancy, Currie, Taylor, Albert Smith, Dimmer, McGibbons, Gemmell and Torbet.
Scorer: Terry McGibbons.

Game 12. 24th October, 1936, Somerset Park:
Ayr United 4 Alloa Athletic 0.
Team: Bob Smith, Bourhill, Strain, Clancy, Currie, Taylor, Albert Smith, Dimmer, McGibbons, Gemmell and Torbet.
Scorers: Terry McGibbons 3 and David Gemmell.

Game 13. 31st October, 1936, Somerset Park:
Ayr United 8 Brechin City 1.
Team: Bob Smith, Summers, Strain, Taylor, Currie, Mayes, Albert Smith, Dimmer, McGibbons, Gemmell and Torbet.
Scorers: John Torbet 2, Hyam Dimmer 4, Terry McGibbons and David Gemmell.

Game 14. 7th November, 1936, Boghead Park:
Dumbarton 1 Ayr United 3.
Team: Bob Smith, Summers, Strain, Taylor, Currie, Mayes, Albert Smith, Dimmer, McGibbons, Gemmell and Torbet.
Scorers: David Gemmell, Hyam Dimmer and John Torbet.

Game 15. 14th November, 1936, City Park:
Edinburgh City 1 Ayr United 4.
Team: Bob Smith, Summers, Strain, Taylor, Currie, Mayes, Albert Smith, Dimmer, McGibbons, Gemmell and Torbet.
Scorers: David Gemmell, Terry McGibbons, Jock Taylor and Albert Smith.

Game 16. 21st November, 1936, Somerset Park:
Ayr United 8 Stenhousemuir 3. Team:
Bob Smith, Summers, Strain, Taylor, Currie, Mayes, Albert Smith, Dimmer, McGibbons, Gemmell and Torbet.
Scorers: David Gemmell, Terry McGibbons 3, John Torbet 3 (including two penalties) and Hyam Dimmer.

Game 17. 28th November, 1936, The Gymnasium Ground:
St.Bernard's 2 Ayr United 5.
Team: Bob Smith, Summers, Strain, Taylor, Currie, Mayes, Albert Smith, Dimmer, McGibbons, Gemmell and Torbet.
Scorers: Terry McGibbons 3 and John Torbet 2 (including a penalty).

Game 18. 5th December, 1936, Forthbank:
King's Park 2 Ayr United 6.
Team: Bob Smith, Dyer, Strain, Taylor, Currie, Mayes, Albert Smith, Dimmer, McGibbons, Gemmell and Torbet.
Scorers: Albert Smith 4, John Torbet and Hyam Dimmer.

Game 19. 12th December, 1936, Somerset Park:
Ayr United 4 Dumbarton 1.
Team: Bob Smith, Summers, Strain, Taylor, Currie, Mayes, Albert Smith, Dimmer, McGibbons, Gemmell and Torbet.
Scorers: Terry McGibbons 2, Albert Smith and Hyam Dimmer.

Game 20. 19th December, 1936, Tannadice Park:
Dundee United 1 Ayr United 2. Team:
Bob Smith, Summers, Strain, Taylor, Currie, Mayes, Albert Smith, Dimmer, McGibbons, Gemmell and Torbet.
Scorers: Hyam Dimmer and David Gemmell.

Game 21. 26th December, 1936, Somerset Park:
Ayr United 8 Montose 1.
Team: Bob Smith, Summers, Strain, Taylor, Currie, Mayes, Albert Smith, Dimmer, McGibbons, Gemmell and Torbet.
Scorers: Hyam Dimmer, John Torbet 2 (including a penalty), Terry McGibbons 3, Albert Smith and David Gemmell.

Game 22. 1st January, 1937, Station Park:
Forfar Athletic 0 Ayr United 5.
Team: Bob Smith, Summers, Strain, Taylor, Currie, Mayes, Albert Smith, Dimmer, McGibbons, Gemmell and Torbet.
Scorers: David Gemmell 2, John Torbet 2 and Terry McGibbons.

Game 23. 2nd January, 1937, Somerset Park:
Ayr United 7 East Stirling 2.
Team: Bob Smith, Summers, Strain, Taylor, Currie, Mayes, Albert Smith, Dimmer, McGibbons, Gemmell and Torbet.
Scorers: David Gemmell 2, Albert Smith, Hyam Dimmer, John Torbet 2 and Terry McGibbons.

Game 24. 9th January, 1937, Meadowbank:
Leith Athletic 3 Ayr United 2.
Team: Bob Smith, Summers, Strain, Taylor, Currie, Mayes, Albert Smith, Dimmer, McGibbons, Gemmell and Torbet.
Scorers: Terry McGibbons and John Torbet.

Game 25. 16th January, 1937, Somerset Park:
Ayr United 1 Raith Rovers 0.
Team: Bob Smith, Summers, Strain, Dyer, Currie, Mayes, Albert Smith, Dimmer, McGibbons, Gemmell and Torbet.
Scorer: David Gemmell.

Game 26. 23rd January, 1937, Glebe Park:
Brechin City 2 Ayr United 3.
Team: Bob Smith, Summers, Strain, Allan, Currie, Mayes, Albert Smith, Dimmer, McGibbons, Gemmell and Newall.
Scorer: Terry McGibbons 3 (including a penalty).

Game 27. 6th February, 1937, Somerset Park:
Ayr United 2 Cowdenbeath 0.
Team: Bob Smith, Summers, Strain, Taylor, Currie, Mayes, Albert Smith, Dimmer, McGibbons, Gemmell and Torbet.
Scorers: Hyam Dimmer and John Torbet.

Game 28. 13th February, 1937, Somerset Park:
Ayr United 5 St.Bernard's 2.
Team: Bob Smith, Summers, Strain, Taylor, Currie, Mayes, Albert Smith, Dimmer, McGibbons, Gemmell and Torbet.
Scorers: Hyam Dimmer 2, Jock Taylor, Albert Smith and Terry McGibbons.

Game 29. 20th February, 1937, Somerset Park:
Ayr United 5 Airdrie 2.
Team: Bob Smith, Summers, Strain, Taylor, Currie, Mayes, Albert Smith, Dimmer, McGibbons, Gemmell and Torbet.
Scorers: Terry McGibbons 3, Hyam Dimmer and Albert Smith.

Game 30. 6th March, 1937, Recreation Park:
Alloa Athletic 1 Ayr United 4.
Team: Bob Smith, Summers, Strain, Taylor, Currie, Mayes, Albert Smith, Dimmer, McGibbons, Gemmell and Torbet.
Scorers: John Torbet (penalty), Albert Smith, Terry McGibbons and Hyam Dimmer.

Game 31. 20th March, 1937, Somerset Park:
Ayr United 1 Morton 1.
Team: Bob Smith, Summers, Strain, Taylor, Currie, Mayes, Albert Smith, Dimmer, McGibbons, Gemmell and Torbet.
Scorer: Maley – own goal.

Game 32. 27th March, 1937, Somerset Park:
Ayr United 5 King's Park 0.
Team: Bob Smith, Summers, Strain, Taylor, Currie, Mayes, Albert Smith, Dimmer, McGibbons, Gemmell and Torbet.
Scorers: Hyam Dimmer 2, Terry McGibbons 2 and David Gemmell.

Game 33. 3rd April, 1937, Stark's Park:
Raith Rovers 2 Ayr United 2.
Team: Bob Smith, Summers, Strain, Taylor, Currie, Mayes, Albert Smith, Dimmer, McGibbons, Gemmell and Torbet.
Scorers: John Torbet and David Gemmell.

Game 34. 16th April, 1937, Bayview Park:
East Fife 4 Ayr United 1.
Team: Bob Smith, Summers, Strain, Taylor, Gray, Mayes, Albert Smith, Dimmer, McGibbons, Gemmell and Torbet.
Scorer: Terry McGibbons.

Second Division top three 1936/37

	P	W	D	L	F	A	Points
Ayr United	34	25	4	5	122	49	54
Morton	34	23	5	6	110	42	51
St.Bernard's	34	22	4	8	100	51	48

League goals

Terry McGibbons	39	William Gibson	1
Hyam Dimmer	25	David Strain	1
John Torbet	22	Maley	
David Gemmell	16	(Morton)	1 own goal
Albert Smith	11	Richardson	
Jock Taylor	3	(Leith Athletic)	1 own goal
Bud Fisher	2	**Total**	**122**

Davy Currie.

Second Division Champions

1958/59
Manager:
Jacky Cox

Ayr United FC in the summer of 1959

In this season Ayr United scored 139 competitive goals to establish what remains a club record. The breakdown comprised 115 in the Second Division, twenty in the League Cup and four in the Scottish Cup. In terms of the league alone, seven more got scored in 1936/37, but in mentioning this there is no intention to detract from this wonderful season of scoring abandon led by Peter Price, Ayr United's greatest player of all time.

In the previous season ninety-eight league goals had been scored for the loss of eighty-one. This was typified by wins of 7-4 (Forfar Athletic at home) and 5-4 (Hamilton Accies away) and a 6-5 defeat (Cowdenbeath away). A 4-3 win at home to Alloa Athletic solicited the following comment in the *Ayrshire Post*: "The sparkle of the teenage forwards was dulled by the depressing display of the defence. The defence quivered at every jab."

In the summer of 1958 Jacky Cox's priority could not have been more clear. The team was possessed of a firepower that gave a strong indication that the goals would continue to flow but defensive frailties had to be addressed. In August Mr Cox signed goalkeeper Ian Hamilton from Kirkintilloch Rob Roy although there was an agreement that he would stay with his Junior club until called upon. He was called up for a first team debut on 20th September and he succeeded in replacing Jim Fulton on a permanent basis.

An attempt was also made to sign Ian Ure, a blonde-haired wing-half with Ayr Albion. Ure opted for Dundee, where he went on to forge a career as a centre-half. He won the league title with Dundee in 1961/62 then went on to have a fabulous career with Arsenal, Manchester United and Scotland.

Losing out on Ure was compensated for by the form of Jim McLean at centre-half. He had been signed from Baillieston Juniors in March 1958 but there was an agreement that he would stay with his club temporarily, because they were in the semi-finals of the Scottish Junior Cup. At the outset of 1958/59 he was free to play. Alex Glen, ex-Dundee, was also acquired and he would prove successful in bolstering the half-back line. Jim 'Tottie' McGhee was a winger signed from Ardrossan Winton Rovers at this time and he remains an Ayr United great.

A pre-season friendly at home to Maybole Juniors afforded little more than shooting practice. Peter Price struck five in a 9-0 romp. Then came the League Cup sectional ties with a group including

Ayr United 6 Alloa Athletic 2.

Hamilton Accies, Montrose and Forfar Athletic. It was safely negotiated. Alas the quarter-final stage was all too formidable. Hearts were the reigning Scottish champions having scored 132 league goals on their way to the title. In September 1958 they had an 8-2 aggregate win over Ayr United in the League Cup knockout stages and they progressed to a final in which they beat Partick Thistle 5-1. It was a mercy that the standard of opposition in the Second Division was considerably less fearsome.

By mid-November twelve league wins had been gained out of the thirteen fixtures. The one blip (2-1 at home to Cowdenbeath in game five) was eminently forgivable. All seven away games had been won and this remains a club record for consecutive away league wins. In reference to a 6-2 home win over Alloa Athletic on 25th October the *Ayrshire Post* noted: "You could almost see the worry on the faces of the Alloa defenders when Price was in possession near goal." One week later the same newspaper, while reporting on a 2-1 win at Dumbarton, noted: "Price was watched like an eagle." In phases of a match he had a tendency to draw his marker all over the field thus creating gaps for his colleagues. Some fans would wrongly interpret this as a tendency to drift out of matches. He knew exactly what he was doing.

"AYR LACK EARLY SEASON SPARKLE" – this headline appeared above a report of a 2-0 home win over Berwick Rangers on 3rd January, 1959. The implication was that anything less than a slaughter was a drop in standards. This headline was rendered redundant over the next three weeks with wins of 5-1 at Cowdenbeath, 8-2 at home to Montrose and 4-0 away to Queen's Park. The third goal against Queen's Park was scored by Alastair McIntyre and it comprised Ayr United's 100th goal of the season including league, League Cup and Scottish Cup. This match was also Ayr United's seventeenth consecutive league match without a defeat and this is still a club record. Mention of this will correctly tell you that fixture eighteen was lost. It is an extraordinary fact that in each of our title-winning seasons there has been at least one exceptionally bad result that defied all logic. In this season it was Ayr United 1 Brechin City 4, Bobby Warrender being the chief tormentor with a hat-trick. The date was 31st January, 1959, and it was the first defeat since 20th September, 1958. Any accusations of lethargy were academic. Full points from the next five league matches left the top of the Second Division looking like this:

By mid-November twelve league wins had been gained out of the thirteen played. This was the only blip. It was a 2-1 loss at home to Cowdenbeath

	P	W	D	L	F	A	Points
Ayr United	28	24	2	2	100	39	50
Arbroath	28	19	4	5	70	45	42

League goal number 100 was scored by Bobby Thomson in the 87th minute of a 4-1 victory at home to Hamilton Accies and it was a remarkable strike from a free-kick at a range of forty yards. With eight games left it was a commanding lead at two points for a win. The Scottish Cup had already ceased to be a diversion after a 2-1 loss at Dunfermline on the last day of February.

A 3-3 draw away to Morton in midweek perhaps had the capacity to delay rather than derail the title push. Ayr United 2 East Fife 0 on the Saturday attracted dreary, but accurate, press comments: "Spectators left the ground early. High scoring is now expected." The same edition of the *Ayrshire Post* further stated: "Ayr United should find little difficulty in making sure of promotion when they meet East Stirling at Falkirk tomorrow." This alluded to the fact that a win at Firs Park was all that was required to secure the club's place in the top flight.

The home team's Andy Boyd was no respecter of reputations. He lodged the ball in the Ayr United net in the 39th minute. Being 1-0 down at half-time was rendered less critical through having the advantage of a strong wind in the second half. The advantage was not taken and time was called on a 1-0 win to East Stirling. Yet promotion was clinched anyway because, on the same afternoon, Dumbarton lost 3-1 at Forfar. Oh the irony that, in such a cavalier season, promotion should be sealed in such an inglorious way. Clinching the title would be similarly inglorious.

Ayr United 3 Forfar Athletic 0 – this took the team to the brink but the fans pitched up short of fever pitch. Considerably short! It was reported that: "There was no enthusiasm amongst the support. It was perhaps due to the absence of a needle." This was understandable. One point was now required to win the league and there were four games left starting with St.Johnstone at Perth. Before the match St.Johnstone manager Bobby Brown congratulated Jacky Cox on his team's success. Three minutes before the end the home team got the game's only goal. It now seemed that a point at Forfar on the following Wednesday would be enough. The operative word is 'seemed'.

On the Monday evening the title was clinched because Arbroath lost to Stenhousemuir. Then, on the next day, the local firm of Lindsay

Ayr United 2 East Fife 0.
Fans felt let down because big wins were expected.

Hicks handed in fifteen dress shirts to Somerset Park. This was to honour a promise made at the start of the season whereby the squad would be presented with a shirt in the event of promotion. Thirteen went to the players in addition to one each for manager Jacky Cox and trainer Eddie Summers.

Two wins and a draw then concluded the season with a club record points total of sixty. This total was eclipsed in 1987/88 by one point in a season in which three more games were played. 1988 was our last title triumph at two points for a win rather than three.

George McIntyre.

Games and Players 1958/59

Game 1. 20th August, 1958, Stair Park:
Stranraer 2 Ayr United 3.
Team: Fulton, Paterson, Telfer, Willie McIntyre, McLean, Glen, Alastair McIntyre, Paton, Price, McMillan and McGhee.
Scorers: Peter Price, Sam McMillan and Jim McGhee.

Game 2. 3rd September, 1958, Ochilview Park:
Stenhousemuir 1 Ayr United 2.
Team: Fulton, Thomson, Telfer, Willie McIntyre, McLean, Glen, Alastair McIntyre, Paton, Price, McMillan and Hendry.
Scorer: Peter Price 2.

Game 3. 6th September, 1958, Somerset Park:
Ayr United 3 Morton 0.
Team: Jim Fulton, Thomson, Telfer, Willie McIntyre, McLean, Glen, Alastair McIntyre, Paton, Price, McMillan and Billy Fulton.
Scorer: Peter Price 3.

Game 4. 13th September, 1958, Shielfield Park:
Berwick Rangers 0 Ayr United 4.
Team: Jim Fulton, Thomson, Telfer, Willie McIntyre, McLean, Glen, Alastair McIntyre, McMillan, Price, Billy Fulton and McGhee.
Scorers: Peter Price 3 and Alastair McIntyre.

Game 5. 20th September, 1958, Somerset Park:
Ayr United 1 Cowdenbeath 2.
Team: Hamilton, Paterson, Telfer, Willie McIntyre, McLean, Glen, Alastair McIntyre, McMillan, Price, Fulton and McGhee.
Scorer: Jim McGhee.

Game 6. 27th September, 1958, Links Park:
Montrose 2 Ayr United 4.
Team: Hamilton, Thomson, Telfer, Willie McIntyre, McLean, Glen, Alastair McIntyre, Paton, Price, McMillan and Fulton.
Scorers: Sam McMillan 2, Billy Fulton and Peter Price.

Bobby Thomson.

Game 7. 4th October, 1958, Somerset Park:
Ayr United 3 Queen's Park 2.
Team: Hamilton, Thomson, Telfer, Willie McIntyre, McLean, Glen, Alastair McIntyre, Paton, Price, McMillan and Fulton.
Scorers: Ron McKinven – own goal and Peter Price 2.

Game 8. 11th October, 1958, Cliftonhill Park:
Albion Rovers 1 Ayr United 4.
Team: Hamilton, Paterson, Telfer, Willie McIntyre, McLean, Glen, Alastair McIntyre, Paton, Price, McMillan and Fulton.
Scorers: Willie McIntyre 2 (including a penalty) and Sam McMillan 2.

Game 9. 18th October, 1958, Glebe Park:
Brechin City 0 Ayr United 4.
Team: Hamilton, Paterson, Telfer, Willie McIntyre, McLean, Glen, Alastair McIntyre, Paton, Price, McMillan and Fulton.
Scorers: Peter Price 2, Sam McMillan and Willie Paton.

Game 10. 25th October, 1958, Somerset Park:
Ayr United 6 Alloa Athletic 2.
Team: Hamilton, Paterson, Telfer, Willie McIntyre, McLean, Glen, Alastair McIntyre, Paton, Price, McMillan and Fulton.
Scorers: Peter Price 4, Billy Fulton and Alastair McIntyre.

Game 11. 1st November, 1958, Boghead Park:
Dumbarton 1 Ayr United 2.
Team: Hamilton, Paterson, Telfer, Willie McIntyre, McLean, Glen, Alastair McIntyre, Paton, Price, McMillan and McGhee.
Scorers: Sam McMillan and Peter Price.

Game 12. 8th November, 1958, Somerset Park:
Ayr United 6 Dundee United 2.
Team: Hamilton, Paterson, Telfer, Willie McIntyre, McLean, Glen, Alastair McIntyre, Paton, Price, McMillan and McGhee.
Scorers: Peter Price 2, Sam McMillan 2 and Jim McGhee 2.

Jim McLean.

Game 13. 15th November, 1958, Somerset Park:
Ayr United 5 Arbroath 2.
Team: Hamilton, Paterson, Telfer, Willie McIntyre, McLean, Glen, Alastair McIntyre, Paton, Price, McMillan and McGhee.
Scorers: Willie Paton, Jim McGhee, Alastair McIntyre 2 and Peter Price.

Game 14. 22nd November, 1958, Douglas Park:
Hamilton Accies 0 Ayr United 0.
Team: Hamilton, Paterson, Telfer, Willie McIntyre, McLean, Glen, Alastair McIntyre, Fulton, Price, McMillan and McGhee.

Game 15. 29th November, 1958, Bayview Park:
East Fife 1 Ayr United 3.
Team: Hamilton, Paterson, Telfer, Willie McIntyre, McLean, Glen, Alastair McIntyre, Fulton, Price, McMillan and McGhee.
Scorers: Willie McIntyre (penalty) and Alastair McIntyre 2.

Game 16. 6th December, 1958, Somerset Park:
Ayr United 4 East Stirling 1.
Team: Hamilton, Paterson, Telfer, Willie McIntyre, McLean, Glen, Alastair McIntyre, Paton, Price, McMillan and McGhee.
Scorers: Alex Paterson, Alex Glen, Sam McMillan and Alastair McIntyre.

Abandoned after twenty-five minutes due to fog.
13th December, 1958, Station Park:
Forfar Athletic 0 Ayr United 0.
Team: Hamilton, Paterson, Telfer, Willie McIntyre, McLean, Glen, Alastair McIntyre, Paton, Stevenson, McMillan and McGhee.

Game 17. 20th December, 1958, Somerset Park:
Ayr United 4 St.Johnstone 2.
Team: Hamilton, Paterson, Telfer, Willie McIntyre, McLean, Glen, Alastair McIntyre, Paton, Price, McMillan and McGhee.
Scorers: Sam McMillan, Peter Price 2 and Jim McGhee.

Jim McGhee.

Game 18. 27th December, 1958, Somerset Park:
Ayr United 4 Stranraer 4.
Team: Hamilton, Paterson, Telfer, Willie McIntyre, McLean, Glen, Alastair McIntyre, Paton, Price, McMillan and McGhee.
Scorers: Alastair McIntyre, Willie McIntyre 2 (both penalties) and Peter Price.

Game 19. 3rd January, 1959, Somerset Park:
Ayr United 2 Berwick Rangers 0.
Team: Hamilton, Paterson, Thomson, Willie McIntyre, McLean, Glen, Alastair McIntyre, Paton, Price, McMillan and Stevenson.
Scorers: Peter Price and Sam McMillan.

Game 20. 10th January, 1959, Central Park:
Cowdenbeath 1 Ayr United 5.
Team: Hamilton, Paterson, Telfer, Willie McIntyre, McLean, Glen, Alastair McIntyre, McMillan, Price, Stevenson and McGhee.
Scorers: Peter Price, Clements – own goal, Jim McGhee, Bobby Stevenson and Alastair McIntyre.

Game 21. 17th January, 1959, Somerset Park:
Ayr United 8 Montose 2.
Team: Hamilton, Paterson, Telfer, Willie McIntyre, McLean, Glen, Alastair McIntyre, McMillan, Price, Stevenson and McGhee.
Scorers: Sam McMillan, Peter Price 2, Bobby Stevenson 2, Willie McIntyre 2 (including a penalty) and Jim McGhee.

Game 22. 24th January, 1959, Hampden Park:
Queen's Park 0 Ayr United 4.
Team: Hamilton, Paterson, George McIntyre, Willie McIntyre, McLean, Glen, Alastair McIntyre, McMillan, Price, Stevenson and McGhee.
Scorers: Jim McGhee, Peter Price and Alastair McIntyre 2.

Game 23. 31st January, 1959, Somerset Park:
Ayr United 1 Brechin City 4.
Team: Hamilton, Paterson, George McIntyre, Willie McIntyre, McLean, Glen, Alastair McIntyre, McMillan, Price, Stevenson and McGhee.
Scorer: Jim McGhee.

Game 24. 7th February, 1959, Somerset Park:
Ayr United 6 Albion Rovers 2.
Team: Hamilton, Thomson, Telfer, Willie McIntyre, McLean, Glen, Alastair McIntyre, McMillan, Price, Paton and McGhee.
Scorer: Peter Price 3 and Sam McMillan 3.

Game 25. 21st February, 1959, Recreation Park:
Alloa Athletic 1 Ayr United 2.
Team: Hamilton, Thomson, Telfer, Willie McIntyre, McLean, Glen, Alastair McIntyre, McMillan, Price, Paton and McGhee.
Scorers: Sam McMillan and Alastair McIntyre.

Game 26. 7th March, 1959, Tannadice Park:
Dundee United 2 Ayr United 3.
Team: Hamilton, Thomson, Telfer, Willie McIntyre, McLean, Haugh, Alastair McIntyre, McMillan, Price, Paton and McGhee.
Scorers: Willie McIntyre, Alastair McIntyre and Willie Paton.

Game 27. 14th March, 1959, Gayfield Park:
Arbroath 1 Ayr United 3.
Team: Hamilton, Thomson, Telfer, Willie McIntyre, McLean, Haugh, Alastair McIntyre, McMillan, Price, Paton and McGhee.
Scorers: Willie Paton, Alastair McIntyre and Jake Young – own goal.

Game 28. 21st March, 1959, Somerset Park:
Ayr United 4 Hamilton Accies 1.
Team: Hamilton, Thomson, Telfer, Willie McIntyre, McLean, Haugh, Alastair McIntyre, McMillan, Price, Paton and McGhee.
Scorers: Sam McMillan, Alastair McIntyre, Jim McGhee and Bobby Thomson.

Game 29. 25th March, 1959, Cappielow Park:
Morton 3 Ayr United 3.
Team: Hamilton, Thomson, Telfer, Willie McIntyre, McLean, Glen, Alastair McIntyre, McMillan, Price, Paton and McGhee.
Scorers: Willie McIntyre 2 (both penalties) and Sam McMillan.

Game 30. 28th March, 1959, Somerset Park:
Ayr United 2 East Fife 0.
Team: Hamilton, Thomson, Telfer, Willie McIntyre, McLean, Glen, Alastair McIntyre, McMillan, Price, Paton and McGhee.
Scorers: Sam McMillan and Jim McGhee.

Game 31. 4th April, 1959, Firs Park:
East Stirling 1 Ayr United 0.
Team: Hamilton, Thomson, Telfer, Willie McIntyre, McLean, Glen, Alastair McIntyre, McMillan, Price, Paton and McGhee.

Game 32. 11th April, 1959, Somerset Park:
Ayr United 3 Forfar Athletic 0.
Team: Hamilton, Thomson, George McIntyre, Willie McIntyre, McLean, Glen, Alastair McIntyre, McMillan, Smith, Paton and McGhee.
Scorers: Jim McGhee 2 and Bobby Smith.

Game 33. 18th April, 1959, Muirton Park:
St.Johnstone 1 Ayr United 0.
Team: Hamilton, Thomson, George McIntyre, Willie McIntyre, McLean, Glen, Alastair McIntyre, McMillan, Price, Paton and McGhee.

Game 34. 22nd April, 1959, Station Park:
Forfar Athletic 1 Ayr United 2.
Team: Hamilton, Burn, George McIntyre, Haugh, McLean, Telfer, Alastair McIntyre, McMillan, Price, Willie McIntyre and Hendry.
Scorer: Peter Price 2.

Game 35. 27th April, 1959, Somerset Park:
Ayr United 3 Dumbarton 1.
Team: Hamilton, Burn, George McIntyre, Willie McIntyre, McLean, Glen, Alastair McIntyre, McMillan, Price, Gibson and McGhee.
Scorers: Peter Price 2 and Jim McGhee.

Game 36. 29th April, 1959, Somerset Park:
Ayr United 2 Stenhousemuir 2.
Team: Hamilton, Thomson, George McIntyre, Willie McIntyre, McLean, Glen, Alastair McIntyre, McMillan, Price, Paton and McGhee.
Scorer: Willie McIntyre and Alastair McIntyre.

Second Division top three 1958/59

	P	W	D	L	F	A	Points
Ayr United	36	28	4	4	115	48	60
Arbroath	36	23	5	8	86	59	51
Stenhousemuir	36	20	6	10	87	68	46

League goals

Peter Price	37	Bobby Smith	1
Sam McMillan	20	Bobby Thomson	1
Alastair McIntyre	16	Clements	
Jim McGhee	15	(Cowdenbeath) 1 own goal	
Willie McIntyre	11	Ron McKinven	
Willie Paton	4	(Queen's Park) 1 own goal	
Bobby Stevenson	3	Jake Young	
Billy Fulton	2	(Arbroath) 1 own goal	
Alex Glen	1		
Alex Paterson	1	**Total**	**115**

Second Division Champions
1965/66
Manager:
Tom McCreath

Ayr United FC 1965/66.

In July 1965 Ayr United manager Tom McCreath said: "We have one ambition and that is to get back into the First Division." At this time it was an outrageously optimistic ambition. Season 1964/65 remains the worst in our history. Finishing second bottom of the Second Division required the club to apply for re-election to the Scottish Football League.

Were there any redeeming features? Well, the biggest cause for gratitude was that the club still existed. In November 1964 the board considered selling the ground to clear debts and to repay shareholders. Closure seemed imminent when it was made known that survival was dependent on the support received from the public of Ayr and district. From personal testimony you can be told that any additional support was unlikely in view of consistently adverse onfield performances. By early January there was a boardroom coup resulting in a vital infusion of capital. The word 'survival' is commonly used in relation to a relegation context. At this time it assumed its literal meaning.

Mr McCreath's stated ambition looked like an impossibility. In the summer of 1965 merely two players got added to what had been a struggling squad. These players were outside-right Johnny Grant, who had been freed by Hibs, and inside-forward Ian Hawkshaw, who had been released by St.Johnstone. Albeit that both would prove to be useful assets, the task ahead would have been daunting for an experienced manager, far less a man who had only played football in minor grades and who, prior to joining Ayr United as reserve team coach in August, 1964, had been involved in the running of Kirkmichael Amateurs. His elevation to club manager in the midst of the financial crisis could only have been viewed as an economical option. Nonetheless the role was maintained for season 1965/66 and his lofty ambition would materialise. He was part-time and his day job was running his joinery business in Maybole. Yet there was a very strong influence lurking in the background. Ally MacLeod had now ceased playing and was very active in a coaching role at the club.

In 1912, 1913 and again in 1928, Ayr United had won the Second Division title without being under the guidance of a manager with strong footballing credentials. It was to happen again under Tom McCreath. Despite the failings of 1964/65 there were players who would benefit greatly from the bitter experience. The 1964 close season signings had included such players as Charlie Oliphant, Eddie Monan, Alex McAnespie, Dick Malone and Arthur Paterson.

The first home match of the league campaign resulted in defeat

Sam McMillan – league winner with Ayr United in 1959/60 and 1965/66.

One year older and a bit more streetwise they were on the point of excelling. Winning at Kilmarnock in the Ayrshire Cup final in April 1965 might also have been a hint of an improved future. Kilmarnock (newly-crowned Scottish champions) 0 Ayr United (just about to apply for re-election) 1 was the result. It was their best ever season and our worst but still they were beaten by a Davy Paterson goal.

The season began in the League Cup section of shame. This was section nine which comprised the five bottom clubs from the previous season's Second Division table. Stenhousemuir (5-2) and Montrose (5-0) were beaten in the first two ties, both at home. The *Ayr Advertiser* contained: "It is our opinion that Saturday TV would be more or less impotent against the counter attraction that a really good Ayr team would offer." The same columns stated: "Already the new spirit has translated itself into bigger gate receipts." Also in the section were Brechin City and Forfar Athletic.

All four games were won but to those supporters of a more cautious nature winning the section was tempered by a concern about how the team would fare when the opposition got tougher. Well, in a supplementary tie for qualification to the quarter-finals Third Lanark were beaten 3-1 on aggregate; this was a club that had just dropped out of the First Division. In the quarter-finals a 2-0 defeat at Kilmarnock could not be overcome in a 2-2 draw in the second leg but there was positivity amongst the fanbase and staff. The improvement from 1964/65 was palpable.

The start to the league programme was low key with a 3-2 midweek win at Montrose. Jacky Coburn got the two goals for the home club. Ten days later he signed for Ayr United. The vagaries of a part-time team playing midweek matches are seldom apparent in a league in which the opposition players also make a living outside of football. However when Ayr United hosted Queen of the South in our first home league match of the season the additional League Cup ties against Third Lanark meant playing Saturday-Monday-Wednesday-Saturday. Queen of the South went home with a 3-1 win and in league fixture three the same margin of defeat was suffered at Cowdenbeath. Sitting sixteenth in a Second Division of nineteen clubs – was this an echo of 1964/65? The league had yet to settle. A scenario of two defeats in three was worked out of the system and one league defeat in the next nineteen propelled the team into title contention. Your writer has a boyhood recollection of the solitary defeat in that run. It took place at Airdrie's Broomfield Park on 13th November, 1965. The

A late defeat but the fans were in good voice

Not what you would call a New Year derby!

Ayrshire Post correctly billed it as: "The key match of the day in the Second Division." There was an outstanding Ayr support. In those days before segregation it could not be equated as a precise number but the proliferation of black and white scarves (no replica shirts in those days!) and the sheer noise in support of the team clearly indicated that the travelling support was heavily more than could have been expected even at a home game one year earlier. Davy Marshall won the game for Airdrie with the only goal which came with six minutes to go. The favoured route from Ayr to Airdrie and back in 1965 was via the Irvine Valley and the memory is still vivid of a virtual convoy of vehicles coming back through Darvel, Newmilns and Galston on that inky black evening. One year earlier the life was being strangled out of the club through lack of support. In mentioning that the fans were back it is a relevant point that some of us were never away in the first place. Throughout those barren seasons of 1962/63, 1963/64 and 1964/65 we were there more in hope than expectation.

Precisely one week before Christmas a 2-1 home win over Arbroath was relevant because it was a victory over the league leaders. It was tightly packed at the top and we had games in hand which assumed a large importance. The title chasing pack now looked like this.

	P	W	D	L	F	A	Points
Arbroath	17	9	6	2	40	25	24
Queen o South	17	9	4	4	37	23	22
Albion Rovers	17	10	2	5	28	20	22
Ayr United	15	9	3	3	33	20	21

January 1966 was a faltering month but not fatally so. Ayr United versus Cowdenbeath was an unconventional fixture for New Year's Day and it took until three minutes from the end for the only goal to be scored. Arthur Paterson poked the ball over the line after an almighty penalty box scramble. It prompted an outburst of joy. In what remained of the month the Ayr United cause was hampered by three 2-2 draws (Queen of the South away, Montrose at home and Berwick Rangers away). These results would have been more damaging in an age when three rather than two points were on offer for a win. In the midst of this we had a 2-0 away win over Albion Rovers.

On the first Saturday in February there was an indication of what might be expected in the event of promotion. In drawing 1-1 at home to St.Johnstone in the Scottish Cup the majority of the 7,346 Somerset Park crowd harboured a sense of injustice. John Murphy went off

January 1966 was hampered by 2-2 draws and this was one of them.

injured early in the tie therefore the majority of it was played with a man short. Losing the replay by a mere 1-0 indicated (wrongly!) that Ayr United would be able to compete in the top sphere.

"The promotion campaign is now reaching a crucial stage. The next four league games are away." This was how the *Ayr Advertiser* of 24th March signposted the way ahead. Alloa Athletic 2 Ayr United 1 – the first in that away run threatened the title hopes in a similar manner to the challenge of 2018. Stranraer 1 Ayr United 5 – Eddie Moore was at his predatory best with a hat-trick. The games at Dumbarton (3-1) and Brechin (2-0) brought further success in the series of road trips. This run of three consecutive wins was extended to seven, the last of which was a 1-0 win at East Stirling on what was an excellent day for Ayr United because Airdrie lost at home to East Fife, Queen of the South lost at Dumbarton and Arbroath only managed a draw at home to Brechin City. In midweek Ayr United 2 Stranraer 2 took the club to the brink of promotion. Three games were left but Alex McAnespie and Ian Hawkshaw were each served with a seven-day suspension with the consequence that their season was over.

An unrelenting schedule was somewhat testing with nine fixtures in April in addition to an Ayrshire Cup tie which doubled up as a testimonial for Sam McMillan. These concluding nine league fixtures were played on Wednesday – Saturday – Monday – Wednesday – Saturday – Wednesday – Saturday – Monday – Wednesday. Being part time the club was at the behest of understanding employers.

```
4.45—CORONATION  STAKES  of
      £2000.  1¼m.
1 SUPER SAM, 4-9-2 ............... J. Lindley
2 PUGNACITY, 4-8-8 ......... W. Williamson
  ALLYMARAIS, 4-8-11 . ... L. Piggott
)¤ 4.46.  Tained  1. Watts.
  runners—1 Say, Ballymarais, Rehearsed,
```

Arbroath 1 Ayr United 1 – promotion was now guaranteed. This had been achieved under the captaincy of Sam McMillan and coincidentally the winner of that day's 4.45 pm race at Sandown was Super Sam. Note too that this happened in the Coronation Stakes. How apt that Ayr United were on the brink of being crowned champions.

Stenhousemuir 0 Ayr United 4 – the title was clinched on the

JAMES McHARRIE (STRANRAER) LIMITED
MOTOR ENGINEERS

County Garage, Stranraer : : Phone 2301 (2 lines)

MORRIS   AUSTIN   RILEY   M.G.   WOLSELEY

B.M.C. SPECIALIST REPAIRERS

You are always welcome to inspect our showroom and have a demonstration run in any car.

Telephone Nos. 2064 and 2619   Telegrams—Buck's Head, Stranraer.

BUCK'S HEAD HOTEL, STRANRAER

LUNCHES, AFTERNOON TEAS and HIGH TEAS

FULLY LICENSED   MODERATE CHARGES

PARTIES CATERED FOR   Manager—Mr W. Muirhead

STRANRAER FOOTBALL CLUB

VERSUS

AYR UNITED

SCOTTISH LEAGUE—SECOND DIVISION

SATURDAY, 26th MARCH, 1966.

3d   Kick-off — 3 p.m.

Official Programme

After the match call at the

"ROYAL"

HANOVER STREET — FOR EXCELLENT FOOD!

Moderate Charges.   Fully Licensed.

Under Personal Supervision of the Proprietor, Mr Pat Burns

PHONE 2035

NORTH WEST CASTLE

A.A.   Home of Sir John Ross — Arctic Explorer   R.A.C.

BEAUTIFULLY SITUATED   ::   FULLY LICENSED HOTEL

Standing in own Grounds.   Unrivalled view of Lochryan.

Luxurious Dining Room   ::   Ship-styled Cocktail Bar

Stranraer 1 Ayr United 5 – our biggest margin of league victory at Stranraer shared with an identical result on 2nd January, 2018.

Monday evening. In the modern age the term 'school night' is used in relation to during-the-week activity. Well for your writer that particular night was a school night in a literal sense but it was a joy to read the morning newspapers. Two nights later it was another school night but, it being a home game, there were no impediments. On a beautiful night, literally and metaphorically, East Fife were beaten 2-0 and it was a thrill to be part of the human tide on the field at the end. The wall was more athletically negotiated in 1966 in comparison to 2018!

Eddie Monan.

Second Division champions 1965/66 Sam McMillan being held aloft

Games and Players 1965/66

Game 1. 25th August, 1965, Links Park:
Montrose 2 Ayr United 3.
Team: Paton, Malone, Murphy, Thomson, Monan, McAnespie, Grant, McMillan, Moore, Hawkshaw and Paterson.
Scorers: Ian Hawkshaw and Eddie Moore.

Game 2. 11th September, 1965, Somerset Park:
Ayr United 1 Queen of the South 3.
Team: Paton, Malone, Murphy, McMillan, Monan, McAnespie, Grant, Kerr, Coburn, Hawkshaw and Paterson.
Scorer: Jacky Coburn.

Game 3. 18th September, 1965, Central Park:
Cowdenbeath 3 Ayr United 1.
Team: Millar, Malone, Murphy, Coburn, Monan, McAnespie, Grant, Davy Paterson, Moore, Hawkshaw and Arthur Paterson.
Scorer: Eddie Moore.

Game 4. 25th September, 1965, Somerset Park:
Ayr United 2 Albion Rovers 0.
Team: Paton, Malone, Murphy, Oliphant, Monan, McAnespie, Grant, McMillan, Moore, Hawkshaw and Paterson.
Scorers: Ian Hawkshaw and Sam McMillan.

Game 5. 29th September, 1965, Somerset Park:
Ayr United 1 Brechin City 0.
Team: Paton, Malone, Murphy, Oliphant, Monan, McAnespie, Grant, McMillan, Moore, Hawkshaw and Paterson.
Scorer: Arthur Paterson.

Game 6. 2nd October, 1965, Station Park:
Forfar Athletic 1 Ayr United 4.
Team: Paton, Malone, Murphy, Oliphant, Monan, McAnespie, Davy Paterson, McMillan, Coburn, Hawkshaw and Arthur Paterson.
Scorers: Jacky Coburn 3 and Davy Paterson.

Dick Malone.

Game 7. 9th October, 1965, Somerset Park:
Ayr United 4 Berwick Rangers 2.
Team: Paton, Malone, Murphy, Oliphant, Monan, McAnespie, Grant, McMillan, Coburn, Hawkshaw and Paterson.
Scorers: Arthur Paterson, Sam McMillan 2 and Jacky Coburn.

Game 8. 16th October, 1965, Hampden Park:
Queen's Park 0 Ayr United 3.
Team: Millar, Malone, Murphy, Oliphant, Monan, McAnespie, Grant, McMillan, Coburn, Hawkshaw and Paterson.
Scorers: Jacky Coburn 2 and Ian Hawkshaw.

Game 9. 23rd October, 1965, Somerset Park:
Ayr United 2 Raith Rovers 2.
Team: Millar, Malone, Murphy, Oliphant, Monan, McAnespie, Grant, McMillan, Coburn, Hawkshaw and Paterson.
Scorers: Sam McMillan and Eddie Monan.

Game 10. 30th October, 1965, Cathkin Park:
Third Lanark 1 Ayr United 1.
Team: Millar, Malone, Murphy, Oliphant, Monan, McAnespie, Grant, McMillan, Coburn, Hawkshaw and Paterson.
Scorer: Johnny Grant.

Game 11. 6th November, 1965, Somerset Park:
Ayr United 2 Dumbarton 0.
Team: Paton, Malone, Murphy, Oliphant, Monan, McAnespie, Grant, McMillan, Moore, Hawkshaw and Paterson.
Scorers: Alex McAnespie and Eddie Moore.

Game 12. 13th November, 1965, Broomfield Park:
Airdrie 1 Ayr United 0.
Team: Paton, Malone, Murphy, Oliphant, Monan, McAnespie, Grant, McMillan, Moore, Hawkshaw and Paterson.

Game 13. 20th November, 1965, Somerset Park:
Ayr United 2 Alloa Athletic 2.
Team: Paton, Malone, Murphy, McMillan, Monan, McAnespie, Grant, Hawkshaw, Moore, Kerr and Paterson.
Scorers: Eddie Moore and Arthur Paterson.

Alex McAnespie.

Game 14. 11th December, 1965, Somerset Park:
Ayr United 5 East Stirling 2.
Team: Paton, Malone, Murphy, Oliphant, Monan, McAnespie, Grant, McMillan, Coburn, Hawkshaw and Paterson.
Scorers: Arthur Paterson, Ian Hawkshaw, Sam McMillan 2 and Johnny Grant.

Game 15. 18th December, 1965, Somerset Park:
Ayr United 2 Arbroath 1.
Team: Paton, Malone, Murphy, Oliphant, Monan, McAnespie, Grant, McMillan, Coburn, Hawkshaw and Paterson.
Scorers: Ian Stirling – own goal and Ian Hawkshaw.

Game 16. 1st January, 1966, Somerset Park:
Ayr United 1 Cowdenbeath 0.
Team: Paton, Malone, Murphy, Oliphant, Monan, McAnespie, Grant, McMillan, Balfour, Hawkshaw and Paterson.
Scorer: Arthur Paterson.

Game 17. 3rd January, 1966, Palmerston Park:
Queen of the South 2 Ayr United 2.
Team: Paton, Malone, Murphy, Thomson, Monan, McAnespie, Grant, McMillan, Coburn, Hawkshaw and Oliphant.
Scorers: Jacky Coburn and Sam McMillan.

Game 18. 8th January, 1966, Somerset Park:
Ayr United 2 Montrose 2.
Team: Paton, Malone, Murphy, Thomson, Monan, Oliphant, Grant, McMillan, Coburn, Hawkshaw and Paterson.
Scorers: Ian Hawkshaw and Jacky Coburn.

Game 19. 15th January, 1966, Cliftonhill Park:
Albion Rovers 0 Ayr United 2.
Team: Millar, Malone, Murphy, Oliphant, Monan, McAnespie, Grant, McMillan, Coburn, Hawkshaw and Paterson.
Scorers: Johnny Grant and Ian Hawkshaw.

Game 20. 29th January, 1966, Shielfield Park:
Berwick Rangers 2 Ayr United 2.
Team: Millar, Malone, Murphy, Oliphant, Monan, McAnespie, Grant, McMillan, Balfour, Hawkshaw and Paterson.
Scorers: John Balfour and Sam McMillan.

Game 21. 12th February, 1966, Somerset Park:
Ayr United 2 Queen's Park 0.
Team: Millar, Malone, McAnespie, Oliphant, Monan, Thomson, Grant, McMillan, Balfour, Hawkshaw and Paterson.
Scorers: Sam McMillan and Alex McAnespie (penalty).

Game 22. 26th February, 1966, Somerset Park:
Ayr United 2 Third Lanark 0.
Team: Millar, Malone, McAnespie, Oliphant, Monan, Thomson, Grant, McMillan, Davy Paterson, Hawkshaw and Arthur Paterson.
Scorers: Sam McMillan and Arthur Paterson.

Game 23. 9th March, 1966, Bayview Park:
East Fife 2 Ayr United 1.
Team: Millar, Malone, Murphy, Thomson, Monan, McAnespie, Oliphant, McMillan, Cummings, Hawkshaw and Paterson.
Scorer: Sam McMillan.

Game 24. 12th March, 1966, Somerset Park:
Ayr United 1 Airdrie 1.
Team: Millar, Malone, Murphy, Oliphant, Thomson, Moore, Davy Paterson, McMillan, Cummings, Hawkshaw and Arthur Paterson.
Scorer: Arthur Paterson.

Game 25. 19th March, 1966, Recreation Park:
Alloa Athletic 2 Ayr United 1.
Team: Millar, Malone, Murphy, Oliphant, Thomson, Moore, Balfour, McMillan, Cummings, Hawkshaw and Paterson.
Scorer: Sam McMillan.

Game 26. 26th March, 1966, Stair Park:
Stranraer 1 Ayr United 5.

Team: Millar, Malone, Murphy, Oliphant, Monan, Thomson, Grant, McMillan, Moore, Hawkshaw and Paterson.
Scorers: Eddie Moore 3 and Ian Hawkshaw 2.

Game 27. 30th March, 1966, Boghead Park:
Dumbarton 1 Ayr United 3.
Team: Millar, Malone, McAnespie, Oliphant, Monan, Thomson, Grant, McMillan, Moore, Hawkshaw and Paterson.
Scorers: Arthur Paterson, Drew Nelson – own goal and Sam McMillan.

Game 28. 6th April, 1966, Glebe Park:
Brechin City 0 Ayr United 2.
Team: Millar, Malone, McAnespie, Oliphant, Monan, Thomson, Grant, McMillan, Moore, Hawkshaw and Paterson.
Scorer: Eddie Moore 2.

Game 29. 9th April, 1966, Somerset Park:
Ayr United 3 Stenhousemuir 0.
Team: Millar, Malone, McAnespie, Oliphant, Monan, Thomson, Grant, McMillan, Moore, Hawkshaw and Paterson.
Scorers: Arthur Paterson, Sam McMillan and Eddie Moore.

Game 30. 11th April, 1966, Somerset Park:
Ayr United 4 Forfar Athletic 1.
Team: Millar, Malone, McAnespie, Oliphant, Monan, Thomson, Grant, McMillan, Moore, Hawkshaw and Paterson.
Scorers: Eddie Moore 2 and Ian Hawkshaw 2.

Game 31. 13th April, 1966, Stark's Park:
Raith Rovers 0 Ayr United 2.
Team: Millar, Malone, McAnespie, Oliphant, Monan, Thomson, Grant, McMillan, Moore, Hawkshaw and Paterson.
Scorers: Sam McMillan and Ian Hawkshaw.

Game 32. 16th April, 1966, Firs Park:
East Stirling 0 Ayr United 1.
Team: Millar, Malone, McAnespie, Oliphant, Monan, Thomson, Grant, McMillan, Moore, Hawkshaw and Paterson.
Scorer: Ian Hawkshaw.

Game 33. 20th April, 1966, Somerset Park:
Ayr United 2 Stranraer 2.
Team: Millar, Malone, McAnespie, Oliphant, Monan, Thomson, Grant, McMillan, Moore, Hawkshaw and Paterson.
Scorers: Eddie Moore and Arthur Paterson.

Game 34. 23rd April, 1966, Gayfield Park:
Arbroath 1 Ayr United 1.
Team: Millar, Malone, Murphy, Oliphant, Monan, Thomson, Grant, McMillan, Balfour, Moore and Paterson.
Scorer: Arthur Paterson.

Game 35. 25th April, 1966, Ochilview Park:
Stenhousemuir 0 Ayr United 4.
Team: Millar, Malone, Murphy, Oliphant, Monan, Thomson, Grant, McMillan, Cummings, Moore and Paterson.
Scorers: Sam McMillan, Arthur Paterson and John Cummings 2.

Game 36. 27th April, 1966, Somerset Park:
Ayr United 2 East Fife 0.
Team: Millar, Malone, Murphy, Oliphant, Thomson, Moore, Davy Paterson, Pullar, Balfour, McMillan and Arthur Paterson.
Scorers: Davy Paterson and John Balfour.

Second Division top three 1965/66

	P	W	D	L	F	A	Points
Ayr United	36	22	9	5	78	37	53
Airdrie	36	22	6	8	107	56	50
Queen o South	36	18	11	7	83	53	47

League goals

Sam McMillan	16	Alex McAnespie		2
Ian Hawkshaw	14	Davy Paterson		2
Eddie Moore	13	Eddie Monan		1
Arthur Paterson	12	Drew Nelson		
Jacky Coburn	9	(Dumbarton)	1 own goal	
Johnny Grant	3	Ian Stirling		
John Balfour	2	(Arbroath)	1 own goal	
John Cummings	2	**Total**		**78**

Second Division Champions

1987/88
Manager:
Ally MacLeod

Champions 1988

Ayr United entered the final league match of 1986/87 requiring a point at home to Stirling Albion in order to win promotion. A win would have been enough to go up as champions in the event of Meadowbank Thistle losing at Alloa. A furious late assault on the Stirling Albion goal was to no avail and the match was lost 3-2. The outcome was a scarcely believable fourth place. It was a day of crushing disappointment. Ally MacLeod was not the type of person to ponder too long on disappointments and his way of dealing with it was to ensure that the next campaign would be one of attacking abandon.

John Sludden had already proven that he could be lethal near goal. At the end of 1986/87 he received the Scottish Professional Footballers' Association Player of the Year award for the Second Division. Then, in June 1987, Tommy Walker, released by Aberdeen, was signed. In making the move to Ayr he was rejecting the interest of St.Mirren and Falkirk. The next important signing came on the eve of the opening league game of 1987/88. Henry Templeton was bought from Airdrie for £6,000. Ally had originally signed him for Airdrie from Shettleston Juniors and, in his final managerial stint, would sign him for Queen of the South from Clydebank. The strike force was complete.

Walker – **T**empleton – **S**ludden – soon to be known as **W**e **T**hree **S**trikers. They stood to get seventy-three league goals between them in the season ahead. In that summer of 1987 goalkeeper David Purdie was still afflicted by a back injury and that was the prompt to sign George Watson from Falkirk. The captain was central defender Ian McAllister who had made his first team debut for Ayr United in the Premier League back on 22nd October, 1977. A good captain leads by example and Cally was a testimony to this. Despite the pain of failing to get the promotion winning point against Stirling Albion he deserved to leave the pitch with his head held high. There were times in that match when he looked as if he was on a one-man mission. His fellow central defender was Willie Furphy, a cool and assured player who was a future Ayr United captain.

Pre-season friendly number one was an 8-0 rout of Annan Athletic at Galabank. The next runout was a 6-0 home defeat which was forgivable against an Arsenal side at full strength. Reading at home was less challenging at 2-2. The league programme was now about to start and Ally had a clear vision not only of his team but the way he wanted his team to play.

WELCOME TO SOMERSET PARK

AYR UNITED

versus

ARSENAL

TUESDAY JULY 28
Kick-Off 7.30pm

•

PROGRAMME 40p

SPONSORED BY AYRSHIRE AND
BURNS COUNTRY TOURIST BOARD

St.Johnstone 0 Ayr United 0 – At the time it was not suspected that this league opener would be against the club that would provide the closest opposition for the title. To those who did not attend the match the result might easily have conveyed a message that it was dull. The opposite was true as mentioned in the *Ayr Advertiser*: "The game had everything in the way of thrills and speedy football despite the score." For the first home league match it was necessary to come from behind to beat Montrose 3-1. Henry Templeton and Tommy Walker excelled yet still the fans could not have anticipated the full extent of what this team was going to unleash on beleaguered Second Division opponents.

Dumbarton's 1-0 Skol Cup win at Ayr in midweek was mired in controversy. We were then left to cling to the argument normally reserved for such occasions: "Oh well, at least we can concentrate on the league." Such sentiments are wearisome at the time yet hindsight tells us that elimination did the club no harm. In the prior midweek victory at Arbroath in the first round had taken place after extra time. Until the onset of the Scottish Cup there would be no such diversions. The focus was clear.

On completion of the eighth league fixture, a 3-0 win at Brechin, Ayr United had scored twenty-three goals for the loss of four. The 6-1 hammering of Cowdenbeath at Central Park on 12th September was the first of eight consecutive league wins. Four of the Ayr goals were timed at 60, 69, 70 and 71. A goal by Henry Templeton in that match had to be seen to be believed. Your writer scarcely believed it, despite witnessing it! He beat three defenders then virtually walked the ball into the net. John Sludden was comparatively sluggish with his hat-trick in eleven minutes. A fortnight earlier he had got a hat-trick in ten minutes in a 5-1 win at home to Stranraer.

On the morning of the Cowdenbeath match there was an uncannily accurate prediction in the columns of the *Glasgow Herald*: "Cowdenbeath, reinforced by recent signings, seem to have tightened up in defence. It is probably just as well for Ayr look ready to take six goals off some team or other before this season is much older." When the prophecy came to fruition, it was the first time we had scored six in a league fixture since 14th October, 1978 (Montrose 4 Ayr United 6).

It was not necessary to wait nine years to score six in a league match again. This time the wait comprised just three weeks. In beating Stenhousemuir 6-0 at Ochilview Park the game was punctuated

WELCOME TO SOMERSET PARK

AYR UNITED
versus
READING

Monday 3rd August, 1987
Kick Off 7.30 p.m.

PROGRAMME 40p

Match Sponsors: DIGITAL EQUIPMENT

with many close scrapes which, with normal luck, could have seen the score edged nearer to double figures. In the closing minutes a Stenhousemuir defender was so harassed that he hammered the ball against his own post, at which point the referee could be seen trying to conceal laughter.

Post match Ally MacLeod voiced one concern. He was worried about the persistent pitch invasions by celebrating fans. The margin of victory equalled the club record for an away league match. That identical 6-0 scoreline had happened at the same ground on 13th October, 1945 and at Berwick on 19th October, 1957. It has happened once since. That was at Cappielow Park on 2nd January, 2001.

From what you have read you will correctly have assumed that top place was occupied. Three more consecutive wins meant that, precisely one third of the way through the league, the statistics were glowing.

	P	W	D	L	F	A	Points
Ayr United	13	11	2	0	39	6	24

In addition to the season's opener the only other drawn match was at Stirling on the historic occasion of the first league match in Scotland to be played on an artificial surface.

The visit of St.Johnstone induced a crowd of 5,168 to Somerset Park and the majority turned up in the hope, or even expectation, of seeing Ayr United stretch the four-point gap to six. Alas, Tommy Coyle deposited the ball in the Ayr net in the 82nd minute and his team mate Ian Heddle did likewise a minute later. Coyle made it 3-0 in the final minute. Allegations of a loss of composure in those closing stages were accurate. This match also signalled the end of a run in which Henry Templeton scored in nine consecutive games to equal the club record set by Peter Price in 1955/56. At the time of writing they still share the record. A contributory factor in the collapse against St.Johnstone was that Ian McAllister was no longer at the heart of the defence having suffered an ankle injury three weeks earlier.

For now at least it was no longer possible to claim that the team had been sweeping everything before it. St.Johnstone trailed by just two points and the situation was aggravated a week later with a 1-0 half-time deficit at Montrose. Ally's supreme powers of motivation worked

Ayr Utd

12th Sept. 1987

Div. 2

when the team took a 4-1 lead with goals timed at 61, 63, 64 and 74. Time was called on a 4-2 win, then there was an unexpected bonus when the results were coming through on car radios. St.Johnstone 0 Cowdenbeath 1 – the four-point lead was re-established.

The notion of a two-club title challenge was questioned by Brechin City three weeks later when they won 2-1 at Somerset Park. That club was now the occupant of second place and the gap amounted to just three points.

Such setbacks were mercifully few in a season in which the fans craved Saturdays. Away from home especially the support was loud and boisterous. It was down to the 'day out' syndrome which still occurs. The support was also numerous and this was a potential difficulty in view of a scheduled trip to play Albion Rovers on 12th December. Originally the plan was to make it all-ticket at Cliftonhill Park with the crowd limited to under 1,000. It was then agreed to switch it to nearby Broomfield Park on a pay-at-the-gate basis. Confidence was probably too high but the feeling of invincibility was gradually eroded in a 1-1 draw which almost ended in defeat. Ross Scott had scored a 61st minute equaliser but with two minutes left he was short with a passback. This allowed Jim Chapman to intercept with a header which beat George Watson and, from where your writer was standing, it looked for certain that the ball was going to end up nestling in the back of the net. Happily it was an optical illusion.

Taking stock of the last two league matches was hardly a positive exercise. One point was taken from a possible four against Brechin City and Albion Rovers, the latter team playing with ten men for the last half hour. The visit of Cowdenbeath then brought a splendid chance to atone, this opinion being borne out by the 6-1 slaughter in Fife when the teams had last met. McKenzie scored in the 13th minute. Was this Paul McKenzie? No he was not in the Ayr squad on this day. Was it Robert McKenzie who had been signed from Maybole Juniors in the summer? No it was not him either. Despite being a scoring sensation at Junior level his Ayr United career would come and go without a first team appearance. In truth the scorer was Cowdenbeath's Alan McKenzie. Worryingly minute after minute after minute went past with all attempts at an equaliser proving abortive. In the 66th minute Ally MacLeod implemented a tactical change which those of us on the terraces thought to be somewhat eccentric. It was soon to prove an act of tactical genius. He took off Tommy Walker,

a striker with an excellent scoring rate thus far in the season, and replaced him with Jim McCann, a defender. Dougie McCracken was then shifted up front with McCann slotting in at the back. McCracken remains an Ayr United cult hero in the mould of Steve Bowey and Jamie Adams in a later age. To become a cult hero it is necessary to be the type of player who would run through a brick wall to advance the Ayr United cause. Here on 19th December, 1987, it could have worked out differently had not Cowdenbeath's Paul Cherry missed an open goal when he really should have made it 2-0 for his team in the 75th minute. Two minutes later Dougie McCracken equalised – he had been a striker for all of eleven minutes. The atmosphere inside the ground was raucous when John Sludden made it 2-1 a minute later. Henry Templeton made it 3-1 three minutes from the end. The *Ayr Advertiser* report carried a headline of: BACK FROM THE DEAD.

"Our best performance of the season" – this was the opinion of Ally MacLeod in response to crushing Stirling Albion 4-0 on Boxing Day. The attendance of 3,658 was favourable for Scottish Football's third tier. In the midst of winning the first five league games of 1988 there was a Scottish Cup elimination against Dunfermline Athletic but one positive spin was that we had a glimpse of Ayr United's drawing power. Drawing 1-1 at a Premier League ground generated so much hope for the midweek replay that a crowd of 11,712 turned up at Somerset Park on a wet night. Losing 2-0 was a disappointment notwithstanding the predictable argument about being able to concentrate on the league.

With Ayr United's style of play the season was littered with sendings-off for opposition players who were driven to desperate means. In each of the ties against Dunfermline, we ended up playing against ten men. Then East Stirling came to Ayr for a 2-0 defeat in which they were reduced to nine men for the whole of the second half. This meant that by the first Saturday in February a total of eight players had been sent off while playing against Ayr United. On the roll of dishonour were Joe Carson (Stranraer), Neil Forbes (Montrose), Graeme Elder (Queen's Park), Derek Edgar (Albion Rovers), John Holt (Dunfermline Athletic), Ross Jack (Dunfermline Athletic), Gary Murray (East Stirling) and John Ward (East Stirling). In the interests of being objective you may be interested to see the list of Ayr United players sent off so far. Players can be modified to player. The only one was Jim McCann in a match at home to Alloa Athletic back on 17th October. With the minutes ticking away in the second half we

Season 1987/88 Issue No. 13 No. 445

ALBION ROVERS

Official Shirt Sponsor
Andrew Dick & Son (Engineers) Ltd.

AIRDRIE & COATBRIDGE ADVERTISER

AIRDRIE & COATBRIDGE ADVERTISER

FINE FARE LEAGUE

40p

FINE FARE SECOND DIVISION

v AYR UNITED

Broomfield Park, Airdrie
Saturday 12th December, 1987
Kick-off — 3.00 p.m.

were trailing to an Allan MacDonald goal. Angus Smith then broke towards goal and would almost certainly have made it 2-0 without the intervention of a professional foul from McCann. Paul McKenzie equalised in the 76th minute and the game was won by a last minute penalty from Henry Templeton. Jim McCann had taken one for the team. At the end of the season the red card count remained at Ayr United 1 Opponents 8.

Berwick Rangers 0 Ayr United 1 was a shock result because many fans expected there to be no result at all. A radio broadcast included the fixture in a list of postponements. Some fans turned back from Edinburgh. Even allowing for atrocious conditions it had been a struggle to grind out a result on a mudbath of a pitch. A comparatively lush Somerset Park offered no excuses when a 1-1 draw was ground out against Queen's Park a week later. Yes, ground out! In the 86th minute Ross Caven struck the Ayr crossbar from close range. It was a dip in form by any definition yet, most fortuitously, our nearest opponents St.Johnstone had an even bigger dip in form by losing at Cowdenbeath. The gap over St.Johnstone was now seven points but they had a game in hand. Had the match at Cowdenbeath gone as expected the gap would have been five with the potential for it to be narrowed to one with their game in hand and the possibility of a win over Ayr at Perth the following Saturday. From the Ayr United perspective the looming match at Muirton Park carried the prospect of opening up a nine-point gap and, at two points for a win, our position would be close to unassailable even allowing for the extra game played. In the event the match was lost 2-0 from first half goals from Kenny Thompson and Mike Smith. To the disappointment of the large visiting support in the 5,190 crowd the normally free flowing Ayr attack was rendered impotent. It took until the second half to get a corner-kick. This result could be put into perspective. It was our first away defeat, in any competition, since losing 2-0 at Arbroath one year and thirteen days earlier.

There is a saying that a week is a long time in politics. It might easily be applied to football. Form was back with a vengeance in a 5-0 slaughter of Cowdenbeath and, with the fans drifting from Somerset Park, the chirpiness was raised to a higher level with the post-match tannoy announcement of Stenhousemuir 3 St.Johnstone 0. When the fans retraced their steps to Somerset Park a fortnight later another scoring binge awaited. In beating Albion Rovers 6-2 it was gratifying

WELCOME TO SOMERSET PARK

AYR UNITED
versus
East Stirling
Saturday February 6, 1988
Kick Off 3.00 p.m.

PROGRAMME 40p

FINE FARE LEAGUE

Match Sponsor: CENTRAL TAXIS, AYR

that such performances were occurring at a perfect time.

One point at Stirling in the next match would guarantee promotion but not yet the title. The importance of the occasion was not lost on the hordes of fans descending on the picturesque Annfield ground. It is true that Stirling Albion had dashed Ayr United's promotion hopes in 1987 but here in 1988 it is doubtful whether anyone even gave that a thought. Contending with a fierce wind and a less-than-refined synthetic surface proved testing factors. Henry Templeton, then Stirling's John Brogan, scored with penalties which left the half-time score at 1-1. The scenes were farcical at the Stirling penalty since the ball kept blowing off the spot. Gusts blowing across a pitch with the texture of a hall floor created a comical interlude although the comical element was lost when the ball was driven beyond George Watson. John Sludden struck six minutes into the second half but John Brogan equalised ten minutes from the end and we had to be content with a 2-2 draw. Content? At the final whistle the mood was somewhere north of mere contentedness. Promotion was now won and the players were soon popping champagne corks in front of fans who were in a state of delirium.

Being pedantic, it could have been argued that promotion had not really been clinched because third-placed Queen's Park had beaten second-placed St.Johnstone that afternoon; with six wins from the remaining six, they could have reached Ayr United's points total of fifty-four. In view of the vast gulf in goal difference this was considered to be an impossible threat. Our +59 stood vastly better scrutiny than the +16 of Queen's Park.

The next target was an obvious one – the title. Yet there was a secondary target. The *Daily Record* had offered a crate of champagne to the first team to score 100 goals in all competitions. When Arbroath were beaten 3-0 at Ayr the total became ninety-seven. To win the prize we had to score three before Rangers scored six. When Stranraer called at Somerset Park it seemed an eminently achievable target but as the game progressed hopes receded. It took until the 37th minute for a breakthrough to be made and, even when it did happen, it came at the wrong end. The scorer was Eric McQueen. Shortly after that goal our former player John McNiven squandered a glorious chance to make it 2-0. As the game progressed into the second half the concern was to win by any score at all. Kenny Wilson (67) and Henry Templeton (77) turned it around and, with the win looking likely, the pressure was on to hit the century. With five minutes left Jim Hughes delivered a cross into the penalty area at the Somerset Road end and John Sludden rose to send a backheader beyond the stricken Martin McLafferty. That brought a 3-1 victory and the prize winning goal. At the final whistle there was a pitch invasion. Then Ally MacLeod and the players appeared in the directors' box to acknowledge the happy fans. Ally MacLeod promised to match the crate of champagne if the team could hit 150. Four games were left!

The fans had decanted east in big numbers to see the promotion winning match at Stirling. Plans were now being made to decant to the same vicinity to see the league title won. A win at Alloa would do it. First of all Ally had to deal with a selection problem. Ian McAllister could not play because of a family bereavement and Willie Furphy was struggling with a hamstring injury. Stevie McIntyre and Jim Hughes comprised the full-back pairing with Robert Brown and Jim McCann in the central defensive role. One week earlier Brown had been playing for East Kilbride Juveniles and now he was appearing in a match in which the Second Division title could be won. Ally MacLeod never had any qualms about throwing young and inexperienced players right in. His motivational powers were supreme. In the 11th minute Henry Templeton was delegated with the responsibility of taking a penalty but in retrospect this was a mistake. Two minutes earlier he had taken a bad knock. Clearly still affected by it, he struck the post from the spot. Suitably stung the Alloa goal was quickly revisited and John Sludden scored with a header in the 13th minute. This was league goal ninety-two and it surpassed Dunfermline Athletic's record of ninety-one in the new-style Second Division. The ensuing rampant attacking yielded a return on the half-hour mark when John Sludden dummied a Kenny Wilson pass to allow Jim Cowell to score. Home goalkeeper Ronnie Lowrie was having a busy shift and he had an outstanding save from John Sludden only to watch in horror as Kenny Wilson drove the loose ball into the net. 3-0 – ten minutes to half-time! The fans were loving it. In the second half the nets were only tested once and that was from a Paul Rutherford penalty so time was called on a 3-1 win. Naturally there was a pitch invasion. This was no easy feat on a quagmire of a pitch and it was an effort to remain acquainted with a whole pair of shoes in the mud. Mathematically the league had not been won but we had a six point lead with three games to play (two points for a win remember) and a goal difference

Ally MacLeod

Champions 1987/88 - Ian McAllister with the trophy.

of +66 in comparison to St.Johnstone's +46. The possibility of not winning the title was so remote that plans were put in place to award the trophy at Somerset Park on the next Saturday. Ninety-four league goals – three games were left to hit one hundred. Sixty points – four points were required to surpass Forfar Athletic's record of sixty-three for the new-style Second Division. Neither of these targets were hit. The incentive was gone.

Ayr United 0 East Stirling 0 was an unexpected result but there were no complaints. After the match the Second Division championship trophy was presented to Ian McAllister and the revelry resumed. The fans were now well skilled in partying. The points total of sixty-one remains a club record based on two points for a win. It was one more than the previous record of sixty in 1958/59. However this statistic should be qualified by letting you know that three more fixtures were played in 1987/88. In the last two fixtures the lethargy was frustrating but understandable. Losing 1-0 to Stenhousemuir was a vast contrast to winning with embarrassing ease at the same ground back in October. The finale was a 2-1 defeat at Brechin on an historic date. 7th May, 1988, was one hundred years to the day since Somerset Park had been opened. It was Ayr FC 3 Aston Villa 0 in the inaugural match.

There was a little more fun to come. Kilmarnock 0 Ayr United 2 in the Ayrshire Cup final would never be forgotten by any of us who were there. Kilmarnock had three players sent off in the last fifteen minutes and the game concluded with the ball being stroked nonchalantly from player to player.

Henry Templeton had the distinction of succeeding John Sludden in being awarded the Scottish Professional Footballers' Association Player of the Year award for the Second Division.

1987/88 was a wonderful season and we had great fun on the way.

Games and Players 1987/88

Game 1. 8th August, 1987, Muirton Park:
St.Johnstone 0 Ayr United 0.
Team: Watson, Hughes, McCann, Furphy, McAllister, Evans, Templeton, McKenzie, Walker, Sludden and Cowell; unused substitutes – McIntyre and McCracken.

Game 2. 15th August, 1987, Somerset Park:
Ayr United 3 Montrose 1.
Team: Watson, Hughes, McCann, Furphy, McAllister, Evans, Templeton, McKenzie (McIntyre), Walker, Sludden and Cowell; unused substitute – McCracken.
Scorers: Tommy Walker 2 and Henry Templeton.

Game 3. 22nd August, 1987, Shielfield Park:
Berwick Rangers 0 Ayr United 2.
Team: Watson, McIntyre, Hughes, McCann, Furphy, McCracken, Evans, Templeton, Scott, Walker, Sludden and Cowell (Wilson); unused substitute – McKenzie.
Scorers: Tommy Walker and Henry Templeton (penalty).

Game 4. 29th August, 1987, Somerset Park:
Ayr United 5 Stranraer 1.
Team: Watson, McIntyre, Hughes, Furphy, McAllister, Evans (McCracken), Templeton, Scott (Wilson), Walker, Sludden and Cowell.
Scorers: Tommy Walker 2 and John Sludden 3.

Game 5. 5th September, 1987, Annfield:
Stirling Albion 1 Ayr United 1.
Team: Watson, McIntyre, Hughes, Furphy, McAllister, Evans (Wilson), Templeton, Scott, Walker, Sludden and Cowell; unused substitute – McCracken
Scorer: Henry Templeton.

Tommy Walker.

Game 6. 12th September, 1987, Central Park:
Cowdenbeath 1 Ayr United 6.
Team: Watson, McIntyre, Hughes, Furphy, McAllister, Evans (McCracken), Templeton, Scott (Wilson), Walker, Sludden and Cowell.
Scorers: Stevie McIntyre, Tommy Walker, John Sludden 3 and Henry Templeton.

Game 7. 15th September, 1987, Somerset Park:
Ayr United 3 Albion Rovers 0.
Team: Watson, McIntyre, Hughes, Furphy, McAllister, Evans, Templeton, Scott, Walker, Sludden and Cowell; unused substitutes – Wilson and McCracken.
Scorers: Jim Cowell, John Sludden and Henry Templeton (penalty).

Game 8. 19th September, 1987, Glebe Park:
Brechin City 0 Ayr United 3.
Team: Watson, McIntyre, Hughes, Furphy, McAllister, Evans, Templeton, Scott, Walker, Sludden and Cowell; unused substitutes – Wilson and McCracken.
Scorers: Henry Templeton and Tommy Walker 2.

Game 9. 26th September, 1987, Somerset Park:
Ayr United 4 Queen's Park 1.
Team: Watson, McIntyre, Hughes, Furphy, McAllister, Evans, Templeton, Scott, Walker, Sludden and Cowell; unused substitutes – Wilson and McCracken.
Scorers: John Sludden 3 and Henry Templeton (penalty).

Game 10. 3rd October, 1987, Ochilview Park:
Stenhousemuir 0 Ayr United 6.
Team: Watson, McIntyre, Hughes, Furphy, McAllister (McCracken), Evans, Templeton, Scott (Wilson), Walker, Sludden and Cowell.
Scorers: John Sludden 2, Jim Cowell 2, Tommy Walker and Henry Templeton (penalty).

Henry Templeton.

Game 11. 10th October, 1987, Somerset Park:
Ayr United 2 Arbroath 0.
Team: Watson, McIntyre, Hughes, Furphy, McAllister (McCracken), Evans, Templeton, Scott (Wilson), Walker, Sludden and Cowell.
Scorers: Tommy Walker and Henry Templeton (penalty).

Game 12. 17th October, 1987, Somerset Park:
Ayr United 2 Alloa Athletic 1.
Team: Watson, McCann, Hughes, Furphy, McCracken, Evans, Templeton, Wilson, Walker (McKenzie), Sludden and Cowell; unused substitute – Welsh.
Scorers: Paul McKenzie and Henry Templeton (penalty).

Game 13. 24th October, 1987, Firs Park:
East Stirling 0 Ayr United 2.
Team: Watson, McIntyre, Hughes, Furphy, McCracken, Evans, Templeton, Scott, Sludden, Wilson, and Cowell; unused substitutes – McKenzie and Kennedy
Scorers: Henry Templeton and John Sludden.

Game 14. 31st October, 1987, Somerset Park:
Ayr United 0 St.Johnstone 3.
Team: Watson, McIntyre, Hughes, Furphy, McCracken, Evans, Templeton, Scott, Walker Sludden and Cowell; unused substitutes – McKenzie and McCann.

Game 15. 7th November, 1987, Links Park:
Montrose 2 Ayr United 4.
Team: Watson, McIntyre, Hughes, Furphy, McCracken, Evans, Templeton, Scott, Walker Sludden and Cowell; unused substitutes – McKenzie and McCann.
Scorers: Jim Hughes, Tommy Walker 2 and Henry Templeton.

Game 16. 14th November, 1987, Somerset Park:
Ayr United 2 Berwick Rangers 0.
Team: Watson, McIntyre, Hughes, Furphy, McCracken, Evans, Templeton (McCann), Scott, Walker, Sludden and Cowell (McKenzie).
Scorer: Henry Templeton 2 (including a penalty).

Ian McAllister.

Game 17. 21st November, 1987, Hampden Park:
Queen's Park 0 Ayr United 2.
Team: Watson, McIntyre, Hughes, Furphy, McCracken, Evans, Templeton, Scott, Walker, Sludden and Cowell; unused substitutes – McCann and McKenzie.
Scorers: Henry Templeton and John Sludden.

Game 18. 28th November, 1987, Somerset Park:
Ayr United 1 Brechin City 2.
Team: Watson, McIntyre, Hughes, Furphy, McCracken, Evans, Templeton, Scott, Walker, Sludden and Cowell; unused substitutes – McCann and McKenzie.
Scorer: John Sludden.

Game 19. 12th December, 1987, Broomfield Park:
Albion Rovers 1 Ayr United 1.
Team: Watson, McIntyre, Hughes, Furphy, McCracken, Evans, Templeton, Scott, Walker, Sludden and Cowell; unused substitutes – McCann and McKenzie.
Scorer: Ross Scott.

Game 20. 19th December, 1987, Somerset Park:
Ayr United 3 Cowdenbeath 1.
Team: Watson, McIntyre, Hughes, Furphy, McCracken, Evans, Templeton, Scott (Wilson), Walker (McCann), Sludden and Cowell.
Scorers: Dougie McCracken, John Sludden and Henry Templeton.

Game 21. 26th December, 1987, Somerset Park:
Ayr United 4 Stirling Albion 0.
Team: Watson, McIntyre, Hughes, Furphy, McCracken, Evans, Templeton, Wilson, Walker, Sludden and Cowell; unused substitutes – McAllister and McCann.
Scorers: Tommy Walker 2, John Sludden and Henry Templeton.

Kenny Wilson.

Game 22. 2nd January, 1988, Stair Park:
Stranraer 1 Ayr United 2.
Team: Watson, McIntyre, Hughes, Furphy, McCracken, Evans, Templeton, Wilson (McCann), Walker, Sludden and Cowell; unused substitute – McAllister.
Scorers: John Sludden and Dougie McCracken.

Game 23. 16th January, 1988, Gayfield Park:
Arbroath 2 Ayr United 4.
Team: Watson, McCann, Hughes, Furphy, McCracken, Evans (McAllister), Templeton, Scott, Walker (Wilson), Sludden and Cowell.
Scorers: Ross Scott, John Sludden 2 and Henry Templeton.

Game 24. 23rd January, 1988, Somerset Park:
Ayr United 3 Stenhousemuir 0.
Team: Watson, McIntyre (Wilson), Hughes, Furphy, McAllister, Evans, Templeton, Scott, McCracken, Sludden and Cowell; unused substitute – Walker.
Scorers: John Sludden, Ross Scott and Henry Templeton.

Game 25. 6th February, 1988, Somerset Park:
Ayr United 2 East Stirling 0.
Team: Watson, McIntyre (McCann), Hughes, Furphy, McAllister, Evans, Templeton, Wilson, Walker, Sludden and Cowell; unused substitute – McKenzie.
Scorers: Ian McAllister and Henry Templeton.

Game 26. 13th February, 1988, Shielfield Park:
Berwick Rangers 0 Ayr United 1.
Team: Watson, McCann, Hughes, Furphy, McAllister, Evans, Templeton, Scott, Walker (Wilson), Sludden and Cowell; unused substitute – McKenzie.
Scorer: Jim Cowell.

John Sludden.

Game 27. 20th February, 1988, Somerset Park:
Ayr United 1 Queen's Park 1.
Team: Watson, McCann, Hughes, Furphy, McAllister, Evans, Templeton, Scott, Walker (McCracken), Sludden and Cowell (Wilson).
Scorer: Tommy Walker.

Game 28. 27th February, 1988, Muirton Park:
St.Johnstone 2 Ayr United 0.
Team: Watson, Scott, Hughes, Furphy, McAllister, Evans (Walker), Templeton, McKenzie (Wilson), McCracken, Sludden and Cowell.

Game 29. 1st March, 1988, Recreation Park:
Alloa Athletic 0 Ayr United 2.
Team: Watson, McCann, Hughes, Furphy, McAllister, Evans, Templeton, Scott, Walker, Sludden and Cowell; unused substitutes – Wilson and McCracken.
Scorer: John Sludden 2.

Game 30. 5th March, 1988, Somerset Park:
Ayr United 5 Cowdenbeath 0.
Team: Watson, McCann, Hughes, Furphy, McAllister, Evans, Templeton, Wilson, Walker, Sludden and Cowell; unused substitutes – McIntyre and McCracken.
Scorers: Kenny Wilson 2, John Sludden, Ian McAllister and Henry Templeton.

Game 31. 12th March, 1988, Links Park:
Montrose 1 Ayr United 1.
Team: Watson, McCann, Hughes, Furphy, McAllister, Evans, Templeton, Wilson, Walker, Sludden and Cowell; unused substitutes – McIntyre and McCracken.
Scorer: Tommy Walker.

Game 32. 19th March, 1988, Somerset Park:
Ayr United 6 Albion Rovers 2.
Team: Watson, McIntyre, Hughes, Furphy (McCann), McAllister, Evans, Templeton, Wilson, Walker, Sludden and Cowell; unused substitute – Welsh.
Scorers: Kenny Wilson 2, John Sludden 2, Tommy Walker and Alan Rodgers – own goal.

Game 33. 26th March, 1988, Annfield:
Stirling Albion 2 Ayr United 2.
Team: Watson, McIntyre, Hughes, Furphy, McAllister, Evans, Templeton, Wilson, Walker, Sludden and Cowell; unused substitutes – McCann and Welsh.
Scorers: Henry Templeton (penalty) and John Sludden.

Game 34. 2nd April, 1988, Somerset Park:
Ayr United 3 Arbroath 0.
Team: Watson, McIntyre, Hughes, Furphy, McAllister, Evans, Templeton (Welsh), Wilson, Walker, Sludden and Cowell; unused substitute – McCann.
Scorers: John Sludden 2 and Jim Cowell.

Game 35. 9th April, 1988, Somerset Park:
Ayr United 3 Stranraer 1.
Team: Watson, McIntyre (McCann), Hughes, Furphy (Welsh), McAllister, Evans, Templeton, Wilson, Walker, Sludden and Cowell.
Scorers: Tommy Walker, Henry Templeton and John Sludden.

Game 36. 16th April, 1988, Recreation Park:
Alloa Athletic 1 Ayr United 3.
Team: Watson, McIntyre, Hughes, Brown, McCann, Evans, Templeton (Scott), Wilson, Walker, Sludden and Cowell; unused substitute – McKenzie.
Scorers: John Sludden, Jim Cowell and Kenny Wilson.

Game 37. 23rd April, 1988, Somerset Park:
Ayr United 0 East Stirling 0.
Team: Watson, McIntyre, Hughes, McCann, McAllister, Evans, Templeton, Wilson, Walker, Sludden and Cowell; unused substitutes –Scott and Brown.

Game 38. 30th April, 1988, Ochilview Park:
Stenhousemuir 1 Ayr United 0.
Team: Watson, McIntyre (McCann), Hughes, Furphy, McAllister, Evans, Templeton (McKenzie), Wilson, Walker, Sludden and Cowell.

Game 39. 7th May, 1988, Glebe Park:
Brechin City 2 Ayr United 1.
Team: Watson, McIntyre (McCann), Hughes, Furphy, McAllister, Evans, Templeton, Wilson, Walker, Sludden and Cowell; unused substitute – Scott.
Scorer: Tommy Walker.

Second Division top three 1987/88

	P	W	D	L	F	A	Points
Ayr United	39	27	7	5	95	31	61
St.Johnstone	39	25	9	5	74	24	59
Queen's Park	39	21	9	9	64	44	51

League goals

John Sludden	31	Dougie McCracken	2
Henry Templeton	23	Jim Hughes	1
Tommy Walker	19	Stevie McIntyre	1
Jim Cowell	6	Paul McKenzie	1
Kenny Wilson	5	Alan Rodgers	
Ross Scott	3	(Albion Rovers)1 own goal	
Ian McAllister	2	**Total**	**95**

Second Division Champions
1996/97
Manager:
Gordon Dalziel

10th May, 1997, at Berwick – Champions.

When the season got underway Ayr United had longer odds to win the title than Berwick Rangers, the club destined to finish in bottom place. The bookmakers probably looked no closer than the completed table for 1995/96. Berwick had finished one place short of the top two promotion slots in comparison to Ayr United's sixth. They had also finished with fifteen points more.

Sixth place in the third tier did not impact unfavourably on the support. In season 1995/96 Ayr United had the highest average home gate in the Second Division. It was a reflection of the momentum which had built up, after a disastrous start that had caused the dismissal of manager Simon Stainrod in favour of Gordon Dalziel. A defeat against Stirling Albion on 4th November, 1995, was our last home defeat of the season. The revived fortunes came too late to make a relevant impact in what was left of the campaign but at least the confidence for 1996/97 was justified.

No Ayr United manager has experienced the concentrated signing activity of Mr Dalziel. Before his arrival the highest turnover of Ayr United players comprised the forty-four who donned the black and white in 1917/18. In season 1995/96 that total was eclipsed by one. Then, in 1997/98, a club record total of forty-six was established. With the subsequent advent of transfer windows it can safely be assumed that this record is safe. For this purpose turnover is defined as the number of players making a first team appearance in a competitive match. The championship season of 1996/97 also involved vigorous recruitment. Sometimes people are apt to look back critically on such high turnover but Gordon Dalziel was a tireless worker who constantly strove for perfection.

From now on linesmen were to be known as assistant referees. More than twenty years later we can reflect that the change of title was ignored by fans. This time also coincided with a change of club captain. Ronnie Coyle was given the appointment in place of Willie Jamieson who lived in Edinburgh therefore he was in at the ground less often. Recruitment was prolific. Teenagers Phil Taylor and Scott Hewitt were signed from Blackburn Rovers and they were joined by Jim Mercer and Colin Smith who were signed from Campsie Black Watch.

These were fringe players but Stevie Kerrigan would ascend to a loftier status. The 23-year-old striker was formerly of Albion Rovers, Clydebank and, more recently, Stranraer. Gordon Dalziel had tried

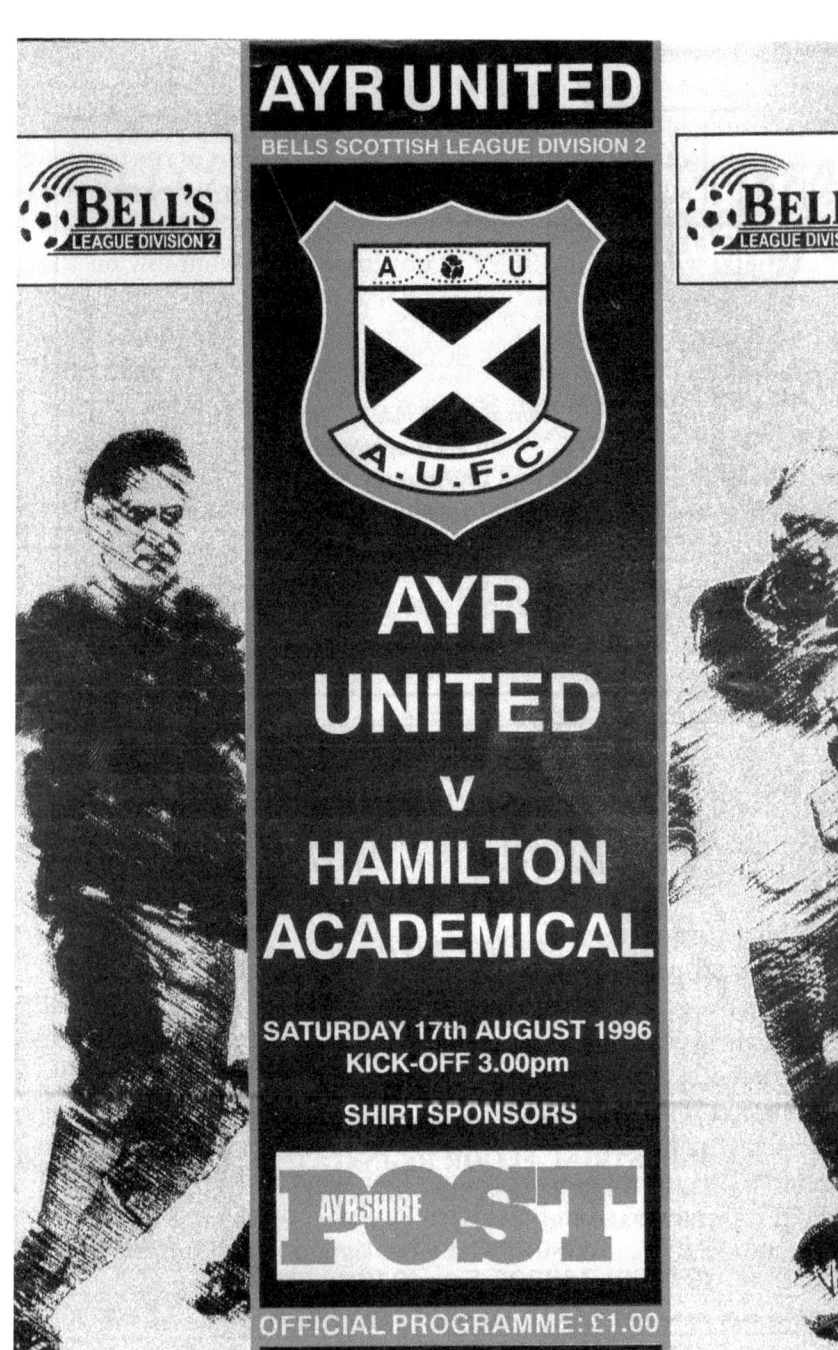

Alain Horace in action against Hamilton Accies on 26th April, 1997.

to sign him during season 1995/96 but he had been acquired for Stranraer just an hour earlier. Now that he had been secured the vision was that he would forge a lethal striking partnership with Isaac English. Goalkeeper Justin Cameron was another of the fringe players signed at this time. He had been on the books at Wimbledon and his boyhood hero was Henry Smith who would now be his mentor at Ayr. Yet Willie McCulloch had a stronger claim for the gloves than young Cameron. The signing of attack-minded midfielder Paul Smith got delayed until Hearts boss Jim Jefferies got back from holiday. It was a worthwhile wait.

Pre-season training was energetic. With athlete Brian Whittle assisting it could have been no other way. When Luton Town came to Ayr for a friendly it could be seen that stamina was not lacking. The only goal of the match was scored by Stevie Kerrigan. Next up at Ayr came Millwall who just happened to be managed by Jimmy Nicholl, Gordon Dalziel's former boss at Raith Rovers. Gregg Hood, Stevie Kerrigan (2) and Isaac English scored in a 4-3 win. It was 4-0 at one stage and at 4-1 Paul Kinnaird missed a penalty. Stevie Crawford got a hat-trick as if to compound the Raith connections. So who came to Ayr for the next friendly? Raith Rovers – although you had probably guessed. A 4-0 defeat solicited the following comment from Gordon Dalziel: "This kick in the pants will do us the world of good."

The "kick in the pants" manifested itself in a 5-2 home win against Livingston in the season's first competitive match. This was in the League Cup, a competition Ayr United had not scored in since 1991. At 5-1 Paul Smith struck the post. It later transpired that Stevie Kerrigan, who had scored twice, should not have been playing on account of a one-match suspension carried over from his time at Stranraer. The club claimed that there had been no notification of it. What next? Expulsion from the tournament? The verdict was not so drastic. A £12,000 fine was imposed and this was paid by "monies provided from amongst the Board of Directors."

The League Cup reprieve amounted to a massive relief because it was known that Kilmarnock awaited at Rugby Park in the next round. Kilmarnock 0 Ayr United 1 – Robert Connor scored against the club that had freed him. The Ayr support in the 8,543 crowd was jubilant. That support was just as jubilant when Darren Henderson scored an equalising goal at Ibrox in the third round. In an overall crowd of 44,283 our allocation was the entire bottom tier of the Broomloan

Henry in missile horror

BRECHIN are set for an SFA rocket – after a HALF BRICK was thrown at Ayr keeper Henry Smith.

Smith was unhurt in the sickening 65th minute incident, with the missile – lobbed from behind his goal – landing in his penalty box.

Police officers – and City vice-chairman David Birse – swooped on the trouble spot instantly in an attempt to grab the madman responsible.

City boss John Young insisted: "This is totally alien in our part of the world and we'll be looking into it."

But the Glebe Park side are bracing themselves for BIG trouble when referee Martin Clark's report arrives at Park Gardens.

Ex-Jambo Smith played down the act of lunacy, but admitted: "You don't expect half a brick to be thrown at you

BRECHIN CITY 1
AYR UNITED 1
By DEREK McGREGOR

89th-minute Craig Farnan

Road Stand. The goal just referred to was the club's 500th in the history of the League Cup competition but, alas, it wasn't decisive since Rangers won by a flattering 3-1 scoreline. By this time we had already exited the Challenge Cup, a tournament neither the fans nor players could muster much enthusiasm for. In losing 4-0 at home to St.Johnstone the Ayr team was below strength. A more pressing concern was that the league programme was already underway.

The opening league fixture was a 1-1 draw at home to Hamilton Accies but even the most minor attention paid to statistical analysis would have indicated that this would be the result. Of Ayr United's last seven opening league games, including this one, five had been at home and all five had ended 1-1. The run of eight winless opening league games from 1992 until 1999 inclusive is a club record. It was written in the statistics that we would not get off to a flyer in 1996.

Glebe Park is not a ground reputed for enflamed passions but, in an ill-tempered 1-1 draw at Brechin, a half-brick was thrown at Henry Smith. Neither is it a ground with fond memories for Duncan George. On 5th February, 1994, as a result of an awful tackle from Ralph Brand, he was stretchered off just eight minutes into a 4-1 win at that ground. It ended his season. Here on 24th August, 1996, he got sent off two minutes before half-time for lashing out in retaliation at Dougie Scott. Our next visit to Glebe Park was on 22nd February, 1997, on which date Duncan got sent off in the 79th minute of a 1-1 draw. The fact that the red card was for a tackle on Ralph Brand could lead to the conclusion that it was an attempt at revenge. However, it was a 50/50 challenge, and it incurred a five-match ban.

This was the first season in which Ayr United would win a title when three points, rather than two, were on offer for a win. In the context of two points taken from the available six it could have been perceived that the expected momentum from 1995/96 had failed to materialise. Yet to put a positive spin on the issue of context it could have been equally perceived that the league programme was barely underway.

Ayr United 6 Berwick Rangers 0 – now we had a sign that the challenge was serious. Gordon Dalziel stated: "I wasn't too bothered about Monday night's Challenge Cup match (versus St.Johnstone). I just couldn't wait for this game. I hope the fans take it the right way but I'd rather get promotion than win cups." In response to the speculation connecting him to the managerial vacancy at Raith

John Traynor in action against Hamilton Accies on 26th April, 1997.

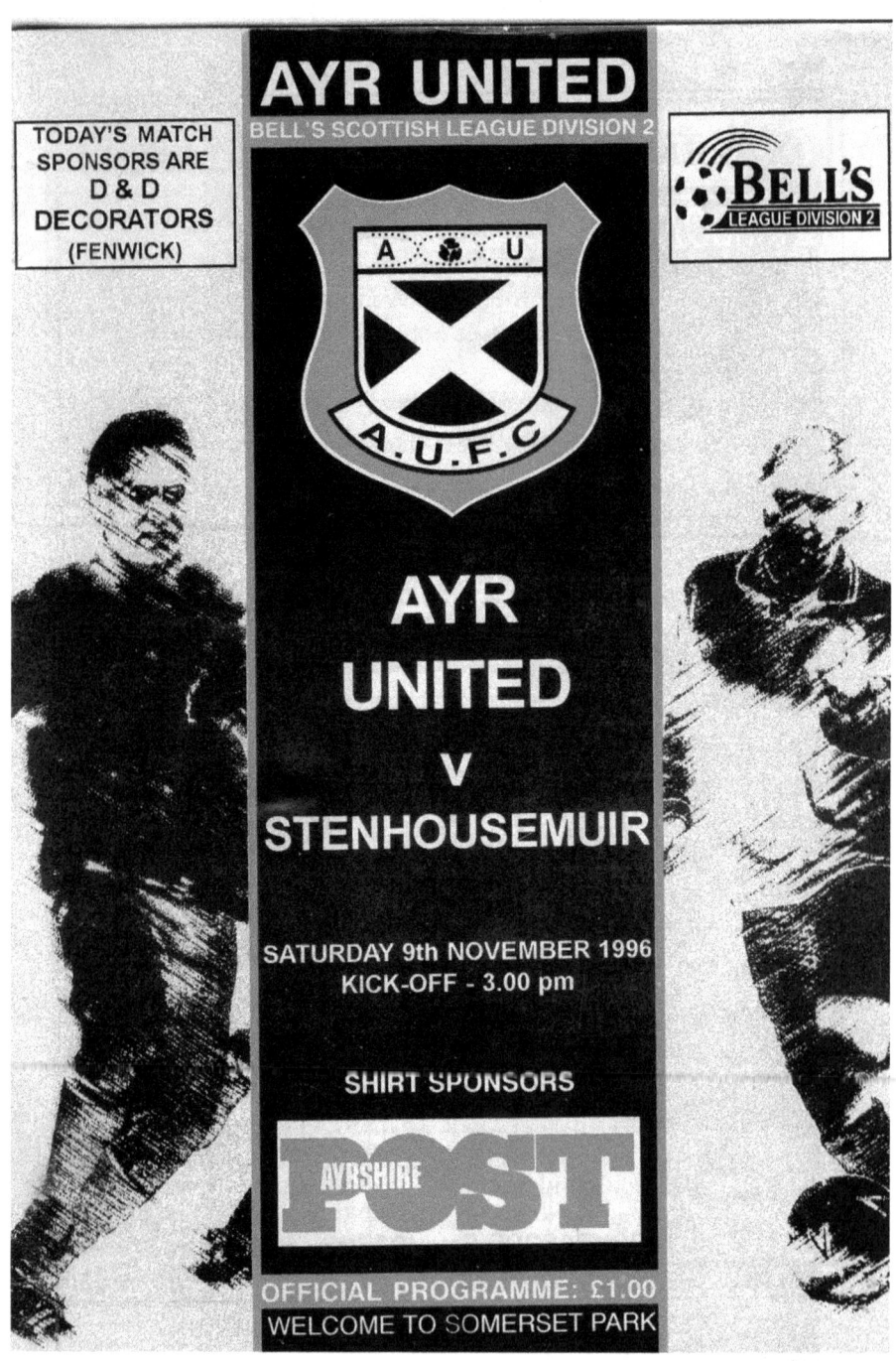

Rovers he was equally candid: "I'm staying here." He had not actually been approached about the job and the vacancy was filled by Tommy McLean who quit after one match then moved to Dundee United to become the manager there. When the Raith Rovers job became vacant again an approach was made to Mr Dalziel and his response was still: "I'm staying here."

A Paul Smith penalty and a last minute winner from Jim Mercer at least got the points away to Stenhousemuir yet there was the inescapable conclusion that it had been a testing fixture. It meant that second place (behind Livingston) was now occupied. The next match was to be a lot more testing. Clyde had not won at Ayr since 16th October, 1971. Midway through the second half that particular statistic was in shreds when Clyde went 4-0 up. Paul Smith and Kevin Biggart succeeded in limiting the damage to 4-2 and shortly after our second goal Jim Mercer had a header cleared off the line. It was our first home defeat in the league since the previous November and compounding the agony we had substitutions for Willie Jamieson and Paul Kinnaird, both with groin injuries. It was anticipated that Jamieson would be out for at least five weeks. His comeback came in nine weeks. Kinnaird was ruled out for "an indefinite period". This was not so ominous as implied. He was listed in the squad for the next match.

Mr Dalziel dismissed the Clyde result as "a hiccup." He was correct. The next seven league fixtures were won to make it our best league run since 1987/88. Queen of the South's Palmerston Park was the venue for the first win in that run and the fans struggled to identify a midfielder in the Ayr United starting line-up. It was Mark Ward. He had played for Oldham Athletic, West Ham United, Manchester City, Everton, Birmingham City and Huddersfield Town. This was his sole Ayr United appearance. After the match he said: "My fitness is so far behind and this is only my third game this term since my pre-season training with Wrexham." The same fixture marked a debut for Paul Watson, a left-back signed from Stirling Albion for a nominal fee. His two-year contract was in sharp contrast to the fleeting Ayr career of Ward.

Match three of the seven-game winning run coincided with a spell of suspension for both Stevie Kerrigan and Duncan George. The match, at Dumbarton, also coincided with the introduction of some oddly-coloured playing garb comprising shirts of green and

Tom Smith unleashes a thunderbolt.

French ace Alain steals it for Ayr

STRANRAER 0
AYR UNITED 1

By ROGER HANNAH

FOR 90 minutes at Stair Park on Saturday I could have sworn I was watching a re-run of Thursday's thrill-a-minute Old Firm clash.

For Celtic, read Stranraer. They had so much possession I had a crick in my neck watching Henry Smith's goalmouth.

For Rangers, read Ayr. They

defender Mark Humphries, helped stem the blue tide. But gaffer Gordon Dalziel wouldn't let him talk to the press about his impressive debut.

And attempts to speak to Horas proved no more successful. His English is little better than my French.

But Dazza had plenty to say and beamed: "I took a big chance bring-

The 24-year-old created the only goal just 17 minutes from the end. His

guys. His English has suddenly come on leaps and bounds – he's shouting 'ya beauty, where's my win bonus?'"

It's been an awful eight days for gutted Blues boss Money. His Challenge Cup winners were hammered by Hamilton then his home was burgled and he put his back out.

He moaned: "Every single time

Darren Henderson in the foreground.

purple halves, shorts of green and purple halves and purple socks. The Marmite principle applied whereby the kit was either loved or hated. There was no such division of opinion over the result. 3-1 to Ayr – we all loved that! With Livingston due at Ayr for the next match the league table assumed a very intriguing aspect.

	P	W	D	L	F	A	Points
Livingston	8	6	2	0	14	6	20
Ayr United	8	5	2	1	19	9	17
Hamilton Accies	8	5	2	1	15	6	17

Tom Smith was signed from Partick Thistle in time to make his debut in the six-pointer which fell on the day of his twenty-third birthday. A ninth minute strike by Robert Connor brought the only goal of the match. It was enough to take over at the top. Livingston then dropped to third since Hamilton Accies had won 2-0 at home to Dumbarton. From one six-pointer we were straight into another – Hamilton Accies away!

At this time Hamilton Accies groundshared with Albion Rovers at Cliftonhill Park which was considered to have a ground limit of 1,238. The crowd of 1,173 was dangerously close to that capacity. For the majority of that number it was a marvellous afternoon – eventually! Seven minutes before half-time Ronnie Coyle conceded a free-kick on the edge of the centre circle. Martin McIntosh took it and it looked as if he was floating the ball into the penalty area. Aided by a strong wind the ball soared long and high before dipping into the net. Consternation – for now! The game changer came in the 62nd minute when Gary Clark scorned a great chance to make it 2-0. Seven minutes later the teams were level. Bobby Law broke down the right then crossed to Stevie Kerrigan who took the ball on his chest then scored with a magnificent volley. Suitably encouraged some sustained pressure on the Hamilton goal ensued and it paid off with the winner five minutes from the end. A Paul Watson cross was neatly brought under control by Isaac English who turned and found the net with a low drive.

It made a great impact on morale to beat our two nearest rivals in consecutive weeks. This was tempered a little by a torn hamstring which had caused Gregg Hood to retire half an hour before the end of the match against Hamilton Accies. It was reported that he would be

The QUEENS

versus
AYR UNITED

5.2.97
Kick off 7.30 p.m.

Tonight's Match Sponsor
**ROBISON
and
DAVIDSON**
"The Builders"

St. Catherines
35-39 Annan Road
Dumfries
Tel: 267423

Programme No. 11
£1.00

sidelined "for a few weeks". If only! It took ten weeks for his comeback. Yet this setback was immediately compensated by the signing of Jock McStay from East Fife. He had been a team mate of Gordon Dalziel and Ronnie Coyle at Raith Rovers. His father's uncle was Willie McStay who played for Ayr United in the 1912/13 title winning season.

Odd-goal victories at home to Brechin and away to Clyde marked the end of the run of seven consecutive league wins. Losing 2-1 at home to Stenhousemuir was deserved on the balance of play but no one could have foreseen such a result. Top position was retained only because Livingston only managed a draw at Brechin.

A reserve match against our Airdrie counterparts was a none too alluring attraction, most especially on a Tuesday evening, but it was rendered significant by virtue of a twenty-four-year-old midfielder who trod the Somerset Park turf as a trialist. He was born in Madagascar but had French citizenship. This was, of course, the multi-skilled Alain Horace, once of Mulhouse. He went straight into the team at Stranraer on the Saturday. Before the match the home team displayed the Challenge Cup which they had recently won and they received warm applause from the Ayr support. This sentimentality gradually evaporated in a match in which the Stranraer defence proved frustratingly difficult to break down. In the 73rd minute Alain Horace scored directly from a corner-kick in what was the pinnacle of an accomplished performance. It was the cue for some of the fans to break from their terracing stance in order to engulf him. It was the only goal of the match and the consequence was that we had scored directly from a corner-kick in consecutive away matches, Paul Kinnaird having performed this feat against Clyde a fortnight earlier. We would complete the season with three goals scored by this means, Paul Smith capping it off at home to Queen of the South on 8th March, 1997. Mark Humphries was another twenty-four-year-old debutant at Stranraer. He had been signed from Raith Rovers.

In the November fixture at home to Queen of the South a consecutive 1-0 win was recorded. It was an unconvincing performance but it amounted to league win number nine out of ten. The mere fact that this statistic has been mentioned is a tell-tale sign that the successful run was on the verge of crumbling. Ayr United 1 Dumbarton 0 – alas this was the half-time score. The full-time result was Ayr United 1 Dumbarton 4. Stevie Kerrigan was sent off six minutes before half-time for supposedly elbowing Jim Meechan. After the game he said

STENHOUSEMUIR FOOTBALL CLUB
Official Match Programme
Season 1996 - 1997   Number 14

Price £1:00

Bell's Scottish League Division Two
Saturday February 15, 1997

STENHOUSEMUIR
v
AYR UNITED F.C.

Ochilview Park Stenhousemuir
Kick-Off 3:00 p.m.

The   CLUB SPONSOR
FOUR IN ONE

WARRIOR

this of the incident: "I put my hand across his body to push him out of the way as I went for the ball. I never used my elbow." Further aggravation was caused by Alain Horace having to go off injured after being afforded no protection from persistent rough treatment.

A trip to Livingston had the potential to either consolidate or lose top place. The latter occurred. After scoring in the second minute the home team posed little more by way of an attacking threat. Isaac English suffered a broken leg in the twelfth minute and he was replaced by John Clark, who was appearing as a trialist (not to be confused with the John Clarke who played for Ayr United in 1995/96).

Clark's appearance meant that he had played in all four of the Scottish leagues on almost consecutive Saturdays. 16th November – his final game for Dunfermline Athletic (versus Raith Rovers) in the Premier League; 23rd November – played for Falkirk (versus St. Mirren) in the First Division and scored the game's only goal in the 89th minute; 30th November – played for Ross County (versus East Stirling) in the Third Division; 14th December – played for Ayr United at Livingston in the Second Division. His late winner for Falkirk counted for nothing.

After the match it was discovered that he was ineligible to play on a temporary basis because he had been a Falkirk player within the year. The result was declared void and Falkirk got fined £25,000. His Ayr United appearance was also on a temporary basis but with no fear of repercussions. No interest was pursued. Prolonged efforts to erase the 1-0 deficit were amply illustrated in one final push which resulted in John Traynor unleashing a fierce drive which Rab Douglas fingertipped against the crossbar. In the entire campaign only two away league defeats would be suffered, both by a slender margin, both at Livingston and both mired in injustice. Here in December Tom Callaghan really should have been red-carded for an horrific challenge on Robert Connor. With twelve minutes left a defender blocked an Alain Horace drive with his arm to spark strong penalty claims which went unheeded.

It was decided to reschedule our fixture with Hamilton Accies from the Saturday before Christmas until Boxing Day. On that particular day Livingston beat Queen of the South 2-1 at home and it was a little daunting to then trail that club by five points albeit with a game in hand. Equally daunting was the impending danger of the Hamilton match. Trepidation was needless. A pitch inspection on Christmas Day ruled Somerset Park unplayable due to frost.

MAIN SPONSORS
OF BRECHIN CITY F.C.

ROWCO INTERNATIONAL PLC

BRECHIN CITY
FOOTBALL CLUB
SEASON 1996-97

**BELLS LEAGUE CHAMPIONSHIP
DIVISION TWO**

BRECHIN CITY

v

AYR UNITED

SATURDAY 22nd FEBRUARY, 1997
Kick off 3.00 p.m.

OFFICIAL PROGRAMME 80p

Definitely not in Duncan George's collection!

On the last Saturday of the year the Hamilton Accies versus Livingston fixture ensured that something had to be conceded in our favour. Even the match postponed verdict was advantageous. Our 2-1 win at Berwick closed the gap with Livingston to two points. Of the three leading clubs only Livingston escaped a postponement on New Year's Day. Livingston 2 Berwick Rangers 2 – a last minute equaliser for Berwick rendered it an even happier New Year in the vicinity of Ayr. Three points off the top with a game in hand was bridgeable.

At this stage Mr Dalziel foresaw problems in attack. Isaac English was recuperating from a leg break and Stevie Kerrigan was due to start a three-game suspension starting on 11th January. To address this he signed striker Robert Scott from East Fife after he had scored a hat-trick in a bounce match against Benburb. On the day after his signing he was ineligible to play in our Tuesday evening Scottish Cup tie at home to Clyde. The tie was lost 2-0, the Kerrigan suspension was now ready to trigger and another suspension was looming since Gregg Hood got sent off in the match.

Nineteen-year-old French goalkeeper David Castilla was given a debut at Dumbarton. He could list Vallauris and Nice as former clubs. In stepping into Henry Smith's position he was replacing a man more than double his age and he was soon to be offered an eighteen-month contract which was eventually extended. At Dumbarton Lee Sharp, a future Ayr United player, scored the only two goals of the match, one an own goal and one an 80th minute equaliser. On the balance of play and in view of how tight it was at the top, a 1-1 draw was not wholly satisfactory but the result had to be measured alongside Livingston's 0-0 draw at home to Clyde and Hamilton Accies' 3-1 defeat away to Stenhousemuir.

Getting detached from the pack would clearly require a step-up in form. Although a rather obvious observation it was nonetheless true. It is pleasing to state that the team delivered this particular requirement. Of the next available eighteen points all eighteen got captured. Two of those games were six-pointers. Those were the visits of Hamilton Accies on a Tuesday night then Livingston on the Saturday. Both were 1-0 victories. The progress stalled a little in a 1-1 draw at Brechin. Duncan George's catalogue of misfortune at Glebe Park has already been documented and his red card in this match got him a five-game ban. Uri Geller had recently tipped Ayr United to win the league. How could we possibly fail?

John Traynor in action against Queen of the South.

There are two documented cases of an Ayr United player being ruled out through toothache. The first was Peter Price at Forfar on 13th December, 1958, although the match got abandoned for fog anyway, and the second was Alain Horace who sat out Ayr United 2 Berwick Rangers 0 on 1st March, 1997. Ayr's most famous son, Robert Burns, was moved to dip his quill into his ink in condemnation of this most terrible malaise.

> *"Where'er that place be priests ca' hell,*
> *Whence a' the tones o'misry yell,*
> *And rankd plagues their numbers tell,*
> *In dreadfu' raw,*
> *Thou, Tooth-ache, surely bear'st the bell*
> *Amang them a'!"*

On the afternoon of the Berwick win the Livingston versus Hamilton Accies fixture got postponed. With precisely three-quarters of our fixtures completed the chances of winning the title looked hugely favourable.

	P	W	D	L	F	A	Points
Ayr United	27	19	4	4	48	25	61
Hamilton Accies	26	14	8	4	44	27	50
Livingston	24	14	5	5	54	23	47

We had the luxury of being able to afford some margin for error but few of us were contemplating error. A swift decisive push was more in our thoughts. Yet the obstacle of stiff opposition rendered this easier said than done. Drawing 2-2 at home to Queen of the South was palatable in the context of our former player Tommy Bryce scorning a great chance for a late winner. It was a matter of relief that his header was uncharacteristically weak.

On his debut at Stranraer in November Alain Horace had scored the only goal of the match in the 73rd minute. In March the story was one of stark similarity when he got the only goal of the match at Stair Park in the 76th minute. A scraped draw and a scraped win was hardly the form of champions but there was a chance to atone at home to Dumbarton. Memories were still vivid of their 4-1 win at Ayr on the last day of November but our next opponents amounted to a struggling

Alain Horace has just scored against Dumbarton.

Paul Smith tangles with the Clyde defence.

team that would ultimately get relegated along with bottom club Berwick Rangers. Light work would surely be made of a team whom we were forty points in front of. Alas football's unpredictability reared its head in a 1-1 draw. Gordon Dalziel commented: "The only plus today was Robert Bell. He came in and put his foot on the ball and made some fine passes." It was a distant echo of 1927/28 when no points were taken off Dumbarton in our successful title quest despite that club finishing eleventh in that season's Second Division.

It was now time to mobilise and head to Livingston and the fans responded to the call in large numbers. The overall attendance of 2,512 contained a loud Ayr United support. A crescendo was reached when Stevie Kerrigan got the ball into the net with a magnificent overhead kick. It was disallowed for a high boot despite no opposition players being in the immediate vicinity. In the 27th minute a corner-kick was delivered by Darren Henderson and met by Gregg Hood who powerfully headed it beyond Rab Douglas for the opening goal. Seven minutes into the second half it was levelled when Henry Smith struggled with a Mark Duthie shot and the ball broke for Grant McMartin to touch it over the line from close range. In stoppage time Livingston's Jason Young was sent clear but there seemed to be nothing to panic over because he was in an outrageously offside position besides which he had brought the ball under control with his hand. Horror of horrors! The referee allowed him to play on and he was left to confront Henry Smith in a one-on-one situation. Young advanced on goal and shot the winner. To the philosophical element of the Ayr support the view was taken that refereeing breaks will even themselves out over the course of the season. However your writer belonged to the faction that left the ground feeling angry at the injustice of what had just happened.

Five games were now left and the gap at the top was three points over Hamilton Accies and nine over Livingston. It was perturbing that our goal difference of +23 bore poor scrutiny in comparison to Hamilton's +40. Stenhousemuir's impending visit had a parallel to the previous home match versus Dumbarton. Once more we would be playing a team that had won at Somerset Park on their previous visit. The match was dominated although this was not reflected in a victory by the slender margin of 2-1. One point was now required to guarantee a top two finish with the consequence of promotion. The next fixture was Clyde away.

Willie Jamieson after scoring against Berwick Rangers on 1st March, 1997.

Mark Duthie in the colours of Ayr United but in 1996/97 he was an opponent with former club Livingston.

In the overall Broadwood Stadium attendance of 1,208 the Ayr support was easily in the majority. On our previous visit back in November the attendance was precisely one person less. The pent-up excitement of going to Stirling for promotion in 1988 was lacking because it was correctly assumed that we were going to finish in the top two anyway and that in itself would be enough for promotion. Fans and players were tempered by a nervousness that the title would be blown. In drawing 1-1 against Clyde promotion was clinched but there was no pitch invasion and the fans were subdued at the final whistle. The mood may have been lifted if Alain Horace had experienced better luck with an 87th minute drive that cannoned back off a post. Gordon Dalziel afterwards commented that Ayr United was a club where the fans do not even celebrate promotion. Hamilton Accies also guaranteed promotion with a 5-0 at Berwick on the same afternoon. Livingston lost 2-1 at home to Dumbarton. Three games were left and the next fixture was Hamilton Accies away. The top of the table that evening was an endorsement of why the champagne at Broadwood tasted flat.

	P	W	D	L	F	A	Points
Ayr United	33	21	7	5	56	32	70
Hamilton Accies	33	21	6	6	73	27	69
Livingston	33	16	9	8	51	37	57

Hamilton Accies versus Ayr United was clearly too attractive a fixture to be played at Cliftonhill Park where the 1,238 capacity would have required a further reduction due to segregation. A switch of venue to Motherwell's Fir Park was vindicated with a crowd of 5,156. The clubs had previously met at Motherwell in the 1991 B & Q Cup final on 8th December, 1991. That tie was lost 1-0 on a day when the team's attitude was called into question. In 1997 there was a buoyancy common to players and fans so this was a day when a strong performance was expected. Fir Park was especially convenient for Gordon Dalziel who stayed a short distance from the ground. In the 28th minute Tom Smith delivered a perfect cross for Robert Scott to score with a header at the back post. To the clear delight of the travelling support that 1-0 lead was still intact at half-time. After the break it was necessary to withstand an onslaught. Paul Ritchie and Steve Thomson both went close during that spell then came a penalty

Stevie Kerrigan (Paul Smith on right) after scoring against Berwick Rangers on 1st March, 1997.

claim after a challenge from Ronnie Coyle on Steve McCormick. The appeals were unheeded but the referee did not feel so charitably disposed when Willie Jamieson pulled down Scott McCulloch. Penalty! Martin McIntosh scored from it. The last seventeen minutes got played out with a dearth of scoring chances for either team but a 1-1 draw suited Ayr United better. Mr Dalziel said: "What we saw today was the crowd potential of Ayr United. They got right behind us today and it was really appreciated." A lead of one point and an inferior goal difference could still have been defined as precarious with two fixtures left yet it was popularly perceived that we had the least difficult of the closing matches.

> To Play: Ayr United versus Brechin City (seventh placed).
> Berwick Rangers (bottom club) versus Ayr United.
> Clyde (fourth placed) versus Hamilton Accies.
> Hamilton Accies versus Livingston (third placed).

Aggravating Hamilton's situation was the fact that Livingston considered the last day fixture to be a grudge match after claiming that they were robbed when the clubs met on 30th March.

The visit of Brechin City attracted a crowd of 3,164, which would assuredly have been higher, had the odds of winning the league been shorter on this day. An Ayr win combined with a Clyde win and it was ours but a favourable result at Broadwood could not be relied upon. Breaking down the Brechin defence required patience. That patience was rewarded in the 36th minute when Willie Jamieson scored with a powerful header from a John Traynor free-kick. At 1-0 there was a strong sense of urgency that a killer goal was required. In the 67th minute it came in explosive circumstances. Goalkeeper Stuart Garden brought down Alain Horace in the penalty area but the referee allowed play to continue and Robert Scott took advantage by rifling the ball into the vacant net. Play was then pulled back, Stuart Garden was sent off and a penalty was awarded. Outfielder Craig Feroz had to deputise as a goalkeeper and the first task of his new role was to fish the ball out of the net after Tom Smith had blasted it beyond him. It remained 2-0 but it was popularly known that Hamilton Accies had beaten Clyde 1-0.

Had the league been won on this day it would have been reminiscent of winning promotion (as runners-up to Queen's Park) in 1956. On

Stevie Kerrigan in action against Queen of the South on 8th March, 1997.

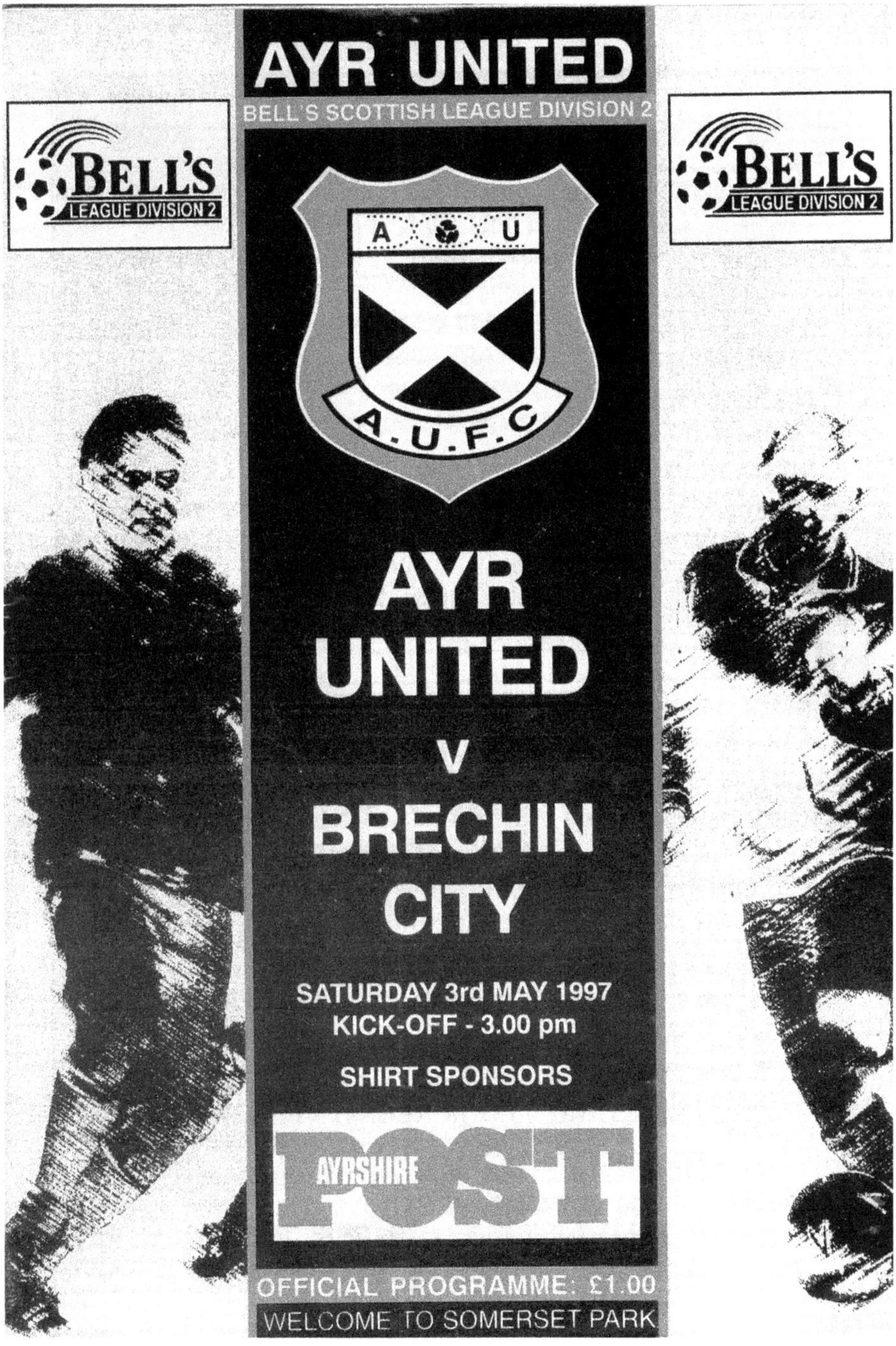
AYR UNITED
BELL'S SCOTTISH LEAGUE DIVISION 2
BELL'S
LEAGUE DIVISION 2
BELL'S
LEAGUE DIVISION 2
A U
A.U.F.C
AYR
UNITED
v
BRECHIN
CITY
SATURDAY 3rd MAY 1997
KICK-OFF - 3.00 pm
SHIRT SPONSORS
AYRSHIRE POST
OFFICIAL PROGRAMME: £1.00
WELCOME TO SOMERSET PARK

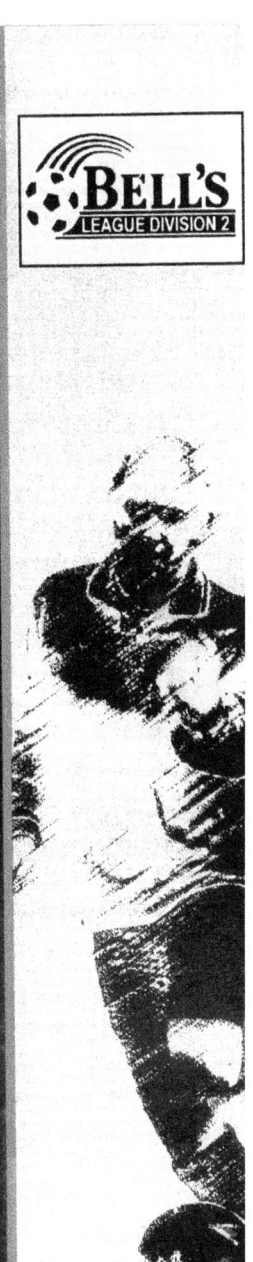

that occasion Brechin City also lost 2-0 at Somerset Park and then, as in 1997, there was a John Traynor in the Ayr United team and a Christie in the visiting team. The 1997 team contained a 21-year-old Robert Bell and in 1956 Ayr United signed a 21-year-old Bobby Bell within a fortnight of the Brechin City match.

Let us return to the topic of 1997. Everything rested on the final day on the ground of Berwick Rangers, the bottom club. The match was approached with a view that only victory would suffice because there was a good possibility that Hamilton Accies would beat Livingston. It transpired that they only succeeded in drawing 0-0, therefore even a draw at Berwick would have sufficed, not that this could have been counted upon.

The match programme showed that the highest league crowd at Shielfield Park to that point of the season had been 564. On this day the attendance was 1,423 and it looked as if somewhere in the region of 1,200 comprised the away support. Four corner-kicks were won in the first five minutes. The home team was being swept aside. Robert Bell, John Traynor and Mark Humphries all got thwarted by the post or crossbar. Chance after chance got scorned and it was frustrating that no breakthrough could be made during such relentless pressure. It was difficult not to contemplate the pressure that would be created if word was to come through that Hamilton Accies had scored. A Berwick fan actually did yell out: "Hamilton have scored."

It was a crude attempt at making mischief. In the 43rd minute Robert Scott had a shot blocked by goalkeeper Michael Burgess. Typical! Not this time though because the ball broke back to him and he fired it into the net. The fans created bedlam. Question: What could be better than a goal just before half-time? Answer: Two goals just before half-time. Possession was quickly regained from the recentre and Tom Smith unleashed an angled drive which the goalkeeper pushed wide but John Traynor was there to cut the ball back for Alain Horace to slam into the net from close range. The fans had still not calmed down after the first goal and the clamour continued throughout the interval. There was a cautious approach in the second half and Henry Smith's goal was rarely threatened.

The celebratory mood regained momentum when time was called on a 2-0 victory. A tannoy warning was heeded. The fans were told that the trophy presentation would not take place in the event of encroachment on the pitch. Ronnie Coyle was then presented with

Paul Kinnaird takes on all comers.

Paul Smith (not in photo) has just scored directly from a corner-kick against Queen of the South on 8th March, 1997.

the trophy in the centre circle. At this time his young son Kevin was seriously ill in hospital and he had already promised the boy a championship medal. Once the presentation had taken place the fans swarmed onto the Berwick pitch in joyous abandon.

At the age of forty-six Ronnie Coyle died on 12th April, 2011. At the peak of his career he had played for Raith Rovers against Bayern Munich in the Olympic Stadium when in direct opposition to Jurgen Klinsmann.

The final points total of seventy-seven remains a club record but our previous title successes had been on the basis of two points for a win rather than three. A significant feature of the 1996/97 success was the formidable manner in which points were accumulated during the run-in. There was only one defeat in the last nineteen league fixtures and, as you have already read, it was a highly contentious one at Livingston. In the absence of that defeat a club record would have been broken but the record for consecutive games unbeaten remains seventeen (1958/59).

Having won the league on the Saturday the trophy was paraded on the Tuesday when Kilmarnock visited in the Ayrshire Cup final. It was a 2-0 win after extra time so we had yet more silver to polish.

Games and Players 1996/97

Game 1. 17th August, 1996, Somerset Park:
Ayr United 1 Hamilton Accies 1.
Team: Henry Smith, Law (Traynor), Hood, Coyle, Jamieson, Connor, Paul Smith, English, Kerrigan, Henderson (Kinnaird) and George; unused substitute – Mercer
Scorer: Isaac English.

Game 2. 24th August, 1996, Glebe Park:
Brechin City 1 Ayr United 1.
Team: Henry Smith, Law, Hood, Coyle (Traynor), Jamieson, Connor, Paul Smith, English (Henderson), Kerrigan, George and Kinnaird (Dalziel).
Scorer: Stevie Kerrigan.

Game 3. 31st August, 1996, Somerset Park:
Ayr United 6 Berwick Rangers 0.
Team: Henry Smith, Law (George), Traynor, Hood (Coyle), Jamieson, Connor, Paul Smith (Mercer), English, Kerrigan, Henderson and Kinnaird.
Scorers: Paul Smith, Isaac English, Stevie Kerrigan 2, Duncan George and Jim Mercer.

Game 4. 7th September, 1996, Ochilview Park:
Stenhousemuir 1 Ayr United 2.
Team: Henry Smith, Law (Biggart), Hood, Coyle, Traynor, Connor, Paul Smith (Mercer), English, Kerrigan (George), Henderson and Kinnaird.
Scorers: Paul Smith (penalty) and Jim Mercer.

Game 5. 14th September, 1996, Somerset Park:
Ayr United 2 Clyde 4.
Team: Henry Smith, Law, Hood, Coyle, Jamieson (Traynor), Connor, George, English, Paul Smith, Henderson (Mercer) and Kinnaird (Biggart).
Scorers: Paul Smith and Kevin Biggart.

David Castilla.

Left to right: Isaac English, Kevin Biggart, Darren Henderson, Ronnie Coyle, John Traynor and Willie Jamieson

Game 6. 21st September, 1996, Palmerston Park:
Queen of the South 1 Ayr United 2.
Team: Henry Smith, Traynor, Watson, Coyle, Hood, Connor, Ward, English, Kerrigan, Paul Smith (Mercer) and Henderson; unused substitutes – Kinnaird and George.
Scorers: Isaac English and Stevie Kerrigan.

Game 7. 28th September, 1996, Somerset Park:
Ayr United 2 Stranraer 0.
Team: Henry Smith, Traynor, Watson, Coyle, Hood, Connor, Paul Smith, English, Kerrigan, George and Henderson (Kinnaird); unused substitutes – Mercer and Burns.
Scorers: Paul Smith and Stevie Kerrigan.

Game 8. 5th October, 1996, Boghead Park:
Dumbarton 1 Ayr United 3.
Team: Henry Smith, Traynor, Watson (Biggart), Coyle (Law), Hood, Connor, Paul Smith, English, Mercer (Colin Smith), Henderson and Kinnaird.
Scorers: Paul Kinnaird, Darren Henderson and Isaac English.

Game 9. 12th October, 1996, Somerset Park:
Ayr United 1 Livingston 0.
Team: Henry Smith, Traynor, Watson, Coyle, Hood, Connor, Paul Smith, English, Tom Smith (Law), Henderson (Mercer) and Kinnaird; unused substitute – Biggart.
Scorer: Robert Connor.

Game 10. 19th October, 1996, Cliftonhill Park:
Hamilton Accies 1 Ayr United 2.
Team: Henry Smith, Traynor, Watson, Coyle, Hood (Henderson), Connor, Paul Smith, English, Kerrigan, Tom Smith (Law) and Kinnaird (Mercer).
Scorers: Stevie Kerrigan and Isaac English.

Robert Scott (right) with Jose Quitongo of Hamilton Accies and Mark Humphries (centre).

Game 11. 26th October, 1996, Somerset Park:
Ayr United 1 Brechin City 0.
Team: Henry Smith, Traynor, Watson, Coyle, McStay, Connor, Paul Smith, English (Mercer), Kerrigan, Tom Smith and Kinnaird (Henderson); unused substitute – Law.
Scorer: Tom Smith.

Game 12. 2nd November, 1996, Broadwood Stadium:
Clyde 2 Ayr United 3.
Team: Henry Smith, Traynor, Watson, Coyle, McStay, Connor (Henderson), Paul Smith (Law), English, Kerrigan (Mercer), Tom Smith and Kinnaird.
Scorers: Paul Kinnaird, Isaac English and Stevie Kerrigan.

Game 13. 9th November, 1996, Somerset Park:
Ayr United 1 Stenhousemuir 2.
Team: Henry Smith, Traynor, Watson, Coyle (Law), McStay, Connor, Paul Smith, English, Kerrigan, Tom Smith (Mercer) and Kinnaird (Henderson).
Scorer: Paul Smith.

Game 14. 16th November, 1996, Stair Park:
Stranraer 0 Ayr United 1.
Team: Henry Smith, McStay, Watson (Henderson), Coyle, Jamieson, Humphries, Paul Smith, English, Kerrigan, Horace (Mercer) and Tom Smith; unused substitute – Traynor.
Scorer: Alain Horace.

Game 15. 23rd November, 1996, Somerset Park:
Ayr United 1 Queen of the South 0.
Team: Henry Smith, McStay (Henderson), Connor, Coyle, Jamieson, Humphries, Paul Smith, English, Kerrigan (Mercer), Horace and Tom Smith; unused substitute – Traynor.
Scorer: Stevie Kerrigan.

Jim Leishman (then manager of Livingston) and Gordon Dalziel.

Game 16. 30th November, 1996, Somerset Park:
Ayr United 1 Dumbarton 4.
Team: Henry Smith, Tom Smith, Connor, Coyle, Jamieson, Humphries, Paul Smith, English, Kerrigan, Horace (Traynor) and Henderson (Mercer); unused substitute – Watson.
Scorer: Isaac English.

Game 17. 14th December, 1996, Almondvale Stadium:
Livingston 1 Ayr United 0.
Team: Henry Smith, Law, Henderson, Traynor, Jamieson, Humphries, Horace, English (Clark), Tom Smith (Paul Smith), Connor and Kinnaird; unused substitute – Watson.

Game 18. 28th December, 1996, Shielfield Park:
Berwick Rangers 1 Ayr United 2.
Team: Henry Smith, Law, Humphries, Hood, Jamieson, Traynor, Paul Smith, Horace, Kerrigan, Connor (Henderson) and Kinnaird (Tom Smith); unused substitute – Mercer.
Scorers: Paul Smith and Alain Horace.

Game 19. 18th January, 1997, Boghead Park:
Dumbarton 1 Ayr United 1.
Team: Castilla, Law, Watson, Traynor, Jamieson, Humphries (McStay), Paul Smith, Horace, Scott, Connor and George (Kinnaird); unused substitute – Dalziel.
Scorer: Lee Sharp – own goal.

Game 20. 21st January, 1997, Somerset Park:
Ayr United 2 Stranraer 0.
Team: Henry Smith, Law, Humphries (Watson), Coyle, Jamieson (McStay), Traynor, Paul Smith, Horace, Scott, Henderson and George (Kinnaird).
Scorers: Willie Jamieson and Robert Scott.

Game 21. 28th January, 1997, Somerset Park:
Ayr United 1 Hamilton Accies 0.
Team: Henry Smith, Law (Hood), Watson, Coyle, Jamieson, Traynor, Paul Smith, Horace (Kinnaird), Scott (Mercer), Henderson and George.
Scorer: Robert Scott.

Isaac English.

Ronnie Coyle

Game 22. 1st February, 1997, Somerset Park:
Ayr United 1 Livingston 0.
Team: Henry Smith, Hood, Humphries (Watson), Coyle, Jamieson, Traynor, Paul Smith, Horace (Kinnaird), Scott, Henderson (Kerrigan) and George.
Scorer: Stevie Kerrigan.

Game 23. 5th February, 1997, Palmerston Park:
Queen of the South 1 Ayr United 3.
Team: Henry Smith, Traynor, Humphries, Coyle, Jamieson, Hood (Kinnaird), Paul Smith, Horace (Watson), Scott, Kerrigan and George; unused substitute – Castilla.
Scorers: Paul Smith, Robert Scott and Stevie Kerrigan.

Game 24. 8th February, 1997, Somerset Park:
Ayr United 3 Clyde 1.
Team: Henry Smith, Traynor, Humphries, Coyle, Jamieson, Hood, Watson, Horace (Kinnaird), Scott, Kerrigan (Law) and George; unused substitute – Castilla.
Scorer: Stevie Kerrigan 3.

Game 25. 15th February, 1997, Ochilview Park:
Stenhousemuir 1 Ayr United 2.
Team: Henry Smith, Traynor, Humphries, Coyle, Jamieson, Hood, Watson, Horace (Tom Smith), Scott, Kerrigan (Paul Smith) and George; unused substitute – Castilla.
Scorers: Duncan George and Robert Scott.

Game 26. 22nd February, 1997, Glebe Park:
Brechin City 1 Ayr United 1.
Team: Henry Smith, Traynor, Humphries, Coyle, Jamieson, Hood, Watson (Henderson), Horace (Paul Smith), Scott, Kerrigan and George; unused substitute – Castilla.
Scorer: Paul Smith.

John Traynor

Game 27. 1st March, 1997, Somerset Park:
Ayr United 2 Berwick Rangers 0.
Team: Henry Smith, Traynor, Humphries (Watson), Coyle, Jamieson, Hood, Paul Smith, Tom Smith, Scott (Kinnaird), Kerrigan and Henderson; unused substitute – McCulloch.
Scorers: Stevie Kerrigan and Willie Jamieson.

Game 28. 8th March, 1997, Somerset Park:
Ayr United 2 Queen of the South 2.
Team: Henry Smith, Traynor, Humphries, Coyle (Watson), McStay, Jamieson, Paul Smith, Tom Smith, Scott (Horace), Kerrigan and Henderson (Kinnaird).
Scorers: Paul Smith and Tom Smith.

Game 29. 15th March, 1997, Stair Park:
Stranraer 0 Ayr United 1.
Team: Henry Smith, Traynor, Humphries, Coyle, Jamieson, Paul Smith, Tom Smith, Horace, Scott (McStay), Kerrigan (Kinnaird) and Henderson; unused substitute – Watson.
Scorer: Alain Horace.

Game 30. 22nd March, 1997, Somerset Park:
Ayr United 1 Dumbarton 1.
Team: Henry Smith, Traynor, Humphries, Watson (Kerrigan), Jamieson, Tom Smith, Paul Smith (Bell), Horace, Scott (McStay), Kinnaird and Henderson.
Scorer: Alain Horace.

Game 31. 5th April, 1997, Almondvale Stadium:
Livingston 2 Ayr United 1.
Team: Henry Smith, Traynor, Humphries, Jamieson, Hood, Paul Smith, Tom Smith (Watson), Horace, Kerrigan (Scott), Henderson and Bell; unused substitute – McStay.
Scorer: Gregg Hood.

Game 32. 12th April, 1997, Somerset Park:
Ayr United 2 Stenhousemuir 1.
Team: Henry Smith, Traynor, Humphries, Hood, Jamieson, Watson, Tom Smith, Horace, Scott (Paul Smith), George and Bell; unused substitutes – McStay and Henderson.
Scorers: Tom Smith and John Traynor.

Game 33. 19th April, 1997, Broadwood Stadium:
Clyde 1 Ayr United 1.
Team: Henry Smith, Traynor, Humphries, Coyle, Jamieson, Watson, Tom Smith, Horace, Scott (Paul Smith), George and Henderson (Kinnaird); unused substitute – McStay.
Scorer: John Traynor.

Game 34. 26th April, 1997, Fir Park:
Hamilton Accies 1 Ayr United 1.
Team: Henry Smith, Traynor, Humphries, Coyle, Jamieson, Watson, Tom Smith, Horace (Kerrigan), Scott (Paul Smith), George and Bell; unused substitute – McStay.
Scorer: Robert Scott.

Game 35. 3rd May, 1997, Somerset Park:
Ayr United 2 Brechin City 0.
Team: Henry Smith, Traynor, Humphries (Kerrigan), Coyle, Jamieson, Watson, Tom Smith, Horace, Scott (Kinnaird), George and Bell; unused substitute – Hood.
Scorers: Willie Jamieson and Tom Smith (penalty).

Game 36. 10th May, 1997, Shielfield Park:
Berwick Rangers 0 Ayr United 2.
Team: Henry Smith, Traynor, Humphries, Coyle, Hood, Watson, Tom Smith (Henderson), Horace (Kinnaird), Scott (Kerrigan), George and Bell.
Scorers: Robert Scott and Alain Horace.

Second Division top three 1996/97

	P	W	D	L	F	A	Points
Ayr United	36	23	8	5	61	33	77
Hamilton Accies	36	22	8	6	75	28	74
Livingston	36	18	10	8	56	38	64

League goals

Stevie Kerrigan	14	Jim Mercer	2
Paul Smith	9	John Traynor	2
Isaac English	7	Kevin Biggart	1
Robert Scott	6	Robert Connor	1
Alain Horace	5	Darren Henderson	1
Tom Smith	4	Gregg Hood	1
Willie Jamieson	3	Lee Sharp	
Duncan George	2	(Dumbarton) 1 own goal	
Paul Kinnaird	2	**Total**	**61**

League One Champions 2017/18

Manager:
Ian McCall

Football leagues are peculiarly branded. When Ayr United won the Second Division in 1987/88 and in 1996/97 it was actually Scottish football's third tier and in 2017/18, when the club again finished on top of the third tier, it was branded League One. The rationale was to make the product more appealing to prospective sponsors. For example League Two has a better resonance than Fourth Division. It was not merely change for the sake of change and neither was Scottish football's introduction (in 1994) of three points for a win rather than two. This was introduced to create an added incentive for attacking football. There was clear justification for this in 2017/18 when Ayr United completed the season having scored twenty-four more league goals than Raith Rovers but, at two points for a win, the latter would have claimed the title. The extraordinary manner of this particular success was the catalyst for this book. It is difficult to conceive of what could have been more extraordinary than the silent wait at the end of the last match.

Relegation from the Championship was a definite source of hurt. To his credit boss Ian McCall assumed accountability: "Since starting out I have never been relegated as either a player or a manager. It's an awful feeling but I take the blame and feel the heat for it." It would seem reasonable that a man who can take the blame when things go wrong would be entitled to take credit when things go right. However when success was achieved in the season ahead Mr McCall modestly deflected the credit away from himself and onto his players. What a guy!

Before departing the topic of giving credit where it is due, an acknowledgement is deserving for the board of directors who boldly announced that the club was reverting to full-time football. This status was a most useful tool in assisting in the recruitment of new players. In the virtual certainty that Nicky Devlin was going to move, the acquisition of Chris Higgins made eminent sense. He was a defender whose Queen of the South contract had just expired. Devlin's anticipated move took him to Walsall. Especially popular was the return of Michael Moffat from Dunfermline Athletic. After three years The Moff was back. He had scored twenty-seven competitive goals for Ayr United in 2013/14 therefore his loss to a rival club was a matter of regret to the fans. Andy Geggan also made the move from Dunfermline Athletic to Ayr United in the summer of 2017. The popular midfield battler had moved in the opposite direction five years previously. Craig Moore's signing was also warmly received

ANNAN ATHLETIC FC

GALABANK, NORTH STREET, ANNAN DG12 5DQ

Betfred Cup
2017-18

Annan Athletic V Ayr United

Saturday 29 July 2017
Kick Off 3:00 pm

For conditions see reverse of ticket

0000055

Ayr United

SPFL

TELEPHONE – 01461 204108   ANNANATHLETIC.ENQUIRIES@BTCONNECT.COM

Betfred Cup

Ayr United
Saturday 29 July 2017
0000055

CONCESSION
To Be Given Up

because he was already a proven striker. He was now our player rather than having Motherwell as his parent club. On one day alone nine players from the Youth Academy signed contracts. Lyle Avci, David Waite, Stuart Faulds, Leon Murphy, Kieran Balfour and Luke McCowan penned full-time deals and James Hilton, Jamie Ballantyne and Grant Thorburn agreed part-time contracts. With key players re-signing and David Ferguson, a defender, joining after his release from Motherwell the squad was ready to go.

Closed-doors friendlies achieve little other than gearing the players up to match fitness and indulging in opportunities to experiment. Partick Thistle 1 Ayr United 5 and Morton 1 Ayr United 4 would have captured backpage headlines in different circumstances. Yet the relevance of such matches should not be totally dismissed. They gave a true reflection of the season ahead since Ayr United would get through the campaign with the highest number of domestic goals of any club in the British senior leagues.

There were never any thoughts of easing into the season gently. The first match was a League Cup sectional tie at home to Kilmarnock. It was all-ticket and BT Sports did a live television broadcast. It became only the second Ayrshire derby to be televised live in its entirety. The other one was the Scottish Cup replay at Rugby Park on 22nd January, 2009.

To accommodate the broadcaster it was switched to the Friday night. 14th July seemed an obscenely early date for a match that meant so much but at least interest in the resumption of football was revived from the off. There was a high degree of optimism in the build-up but it was mainly emanating from Kilmarnock. It must have been blind optimism. Kilmarnock had not won a competitive match at Ayr since 2nd January, 1993. In the seven League Cup ties they had played at Ayr they could only boast one win and even that was as far back as 25th August, 1951. Since their win at Ayr on 2nd January, 1967, the clubs had played twenty-eight competitive matches at Somerset Park (League, League Cup and Scottish Cup). The breakdown was fifteen Ayr wins, five Kilmarnock wins and eight draws. We were now on the point of seeing the statistics tilt even more in our favour.

There was one worry though and, at the time, it did seem very concerning. In Kilmarnock there was a quick clamour for tickets but in Ayr there was no such rush. Stories began to emerge that the visiting support was going to outnumber the home support by three

Mark Kerr, here at Burns' Cottage, signed for Ayr United on Burns Day, 2018.

to one. Gradually the stories became modified to read that the away support would be double. 'Double' then became further diluted to read 'nearly double'. When the game took place it became obvious that these stories were all wayward. The 6,417 attendance comprised an Ayr support of 3,594 and a Kilmarnock support of 2,823. It was a fairly moderate crowd in comparison to derby attendances in the past but it came at a time when many who would have attended were off on holiday while others may have succumbed to the temptation just to watch it on television. In the 38th minute Andy Geggan scored with a header from a Declan McDaid corner-kick. It remained 1-0 and it most certainly could not be said that the home support was humble in victory.

The two-league gap was unapparent on the night and the next sectional tie was at Dumbarton where we were pitched against a team with Championship status. In winning 3-1 the optimists were becoming convinced that a great season would unfold while others more pessimistically took the view that it could be another false dawn. The team then went on to win the section with a 100% record after beating Clyde 5-1 at home and Annan Athletic 6-1 away.

The Annan result created a club record for the biggest away win in the League Cup. Previously there had been a four-way tie: Stirling Albion 1 Ayr United 5 on 16th August, 1947; Third Lanark 1 Ayr United 5 on 28th August, 1956; Partick Thistle 1 Ayr United 5 on 26th August, 1981 and East Stirling 0 Ayr United 4 on 2nd August, 2014. Another club record was broken at Annan. Previously the quickest goal scored by an Ayr United player was from Neil Tarrant at home to Morton on 5th February, 2000. It came in twenty seconds. This accolade now belonged to Ross Docherty who scored at Annan just fifteen seconds after the kick-off. The Annan tie further created another statistic which had no historical precedent. No previous Ayr United team had scored six with six different scorers (although it has happened when we have scored more than six). The nearest historical precedent was a 5-0 league win at Airdrie with five different scorers on 5th March, 2011. At Annan it was possible to renew the acquaintance of a couple of fondly remembered former Ayr players. They were manager Peter Murphy and midfielder Ryan Stevenson.

So what happened next in the League Cup? Indeed what did happen? It was Hibs 5 Ayr United 0 in the lofty sounding round of sixteen. This would be one of only two matches in the entire season

Craig Moore (with the ball) has just scored at Alloa on 22nd April, 2018. To the right are Alan Forrest and Craig McGuffie

in which the opposition would get a clean sheet. We exited the competition having scored fifteen goals, which was a club best in a single season since 1980/81.

The opening league fixture, Albion Rovers away, was entered on a wave of virtual invincibility. Yet some of us were mindful of a similar mood when entering the same ground for a league opener two years earlier only to retreat while grumbling about a 3-0 defeat. Here in 2017 the statistics favoured Albion Rovers. Before this match the clubs had met seven times in an opening league fixture, five at Coatbridge, one at Airdrie and one at Ayr. Five wins for Albion Rovers, one Ayr win and a draw was the analysis. One of the seven, Albion Rovers 5 Ayr United 0 on 12th August, 1939, was later declared void due to the outbreak of war. At least there was one positive consequence of war! The sole Ayr win was a 5-4 victory at Cliftonhill Park on 11th September, 1954. Despite the adverse statistical analysis there was nothing to fear. Albion Rovers 1 Ayr United 5 assumed the proportions of a rout. Declan McDaid scored in the second minute. Having netted the club's first league goal of the season he would also have the distinction of scoring our last league goal of the season and it happened against the same club. Craig Moore got a hat-trick, a feat achieved by Jacky Robertson in the 1954 match just referred to. It was the first opening day hat-trick by an Ayr United player since Ian Whitehead in a 4-1 home win over Dunfermline Athletic on 29th August, 1970. This result in 2017 amounted to our second biggest opening away league win in our history. It was beaten only by Queen's Park 1 Ayr United 6 on 17th August, 1921. It was also the first time an Ayr United team had scored five or more in three consecutive matches since 1953: Albion Rovers 5 Ayr United 6 (league) on 24th January, 1953; Ayr United 5 St.Johnstone 2 (league) on 31st January, 1953 and Buckie Thistle 1 Ayr United 5 (Scottish Cup) on 7th February, 1953.

League fixture number two was at home to Forfar Athletic and it was hoped that confidence would not be dented by the League Cup defeat at Easter Road during the week. At 3-0 the game was comfortably won. Only once previously had Forfar lost at Ayr by this precise scoreline. It had happened on 11th April, 1959, when the club was romping towards the Second Division title? Was this a sign? Probably not. A real sign was the team's form. There was not a strong appetite for competing in the Irn Bru Cup at this stage of the season. On a Wednesday night our tie against Lowland League side East

#SOMERSETPARK

OFFICIAL MATCH PROGRAMME £2

AYR UNITED v STRANRAER
SATURDAY 14th APRIL 2018 | KICK OFF 3.00pm
PROGRAMME NO.20

Ladbrokes LEAGUE 1

bodog

Stirling induced no more than 318 people to Ochilview Park. This put it into the bracket of one of our lowest attendances of all time and it was fortunate that there was an Ayr support of 190. In winning 5-1 this equalled our record winning margin in the Irn Bru Cup and its various manifestations. The record was shared with Ross County 0 Ayr United 4 on 10th August, 1996.

Stranraer 3 Ayr United 4 was one of those matches which was highly exciting in a way that can tend to turn the fans into nervous wrecks. 1-0 down : 3-1 up : 3-3 then a winner five minutes from the end. That winner came from Paddy Boyle and it would prove to be his only goal of the season but ultimately it was vital. Between the League Cup, League One and Irn Bru Cup thirty-two goals had been scored in the nine games played. The last time that number had been exceeded in the first nine games was back in 1911/12. With Arbroath due at Ayr there was an opportunity to have four straight league wins at the start of a season for the first time since 1991/92. The match was lost 2-1 and the consequences were worse than a mere failure to trot out another statistic. Top place was now conceded to Raith Rovers.

There was a quick opportunity to satisfy the lust for goals when Montrose called at Somerset Park for a Tuesday evening tie in the second round of the Irn Bru Cup. Iain Campbell put the visitors ahead in the third minute. Three days earlier his father Dick had masterminded Arbroath's win at Ayr. It was to turn into another triumph for the Campbell clan. After extra time it was tied at 1-1 and Montrose won 6-5 in the shootout. Our two previous shootouts in the competition had been won. Those were against East Stirling away in 1994 and Queen of the South away in 2006. Prior to this Montrose tie we had won six of our seven shootouts at home although in mentioning this it should be made clear that this statistic includes a couple of matches that would fall outside of the definition of competitive football. These winning shootouts at home were versus: Dundee (Scottish Cup) 15/2/2000, Kilmarnock (League Cup) 9th October 2001, Kilmarnock (West Sound Big Match Trophy) 14th July, 2004, Hibs (Ayr Guildry Cup) 16th July, 2005, Hearts (League Cup) 21st September, 2011 and Stranraer (play-offs) 16th May, 2016. Before the Montrose defeat our only losing shootout at Ayr was versus Dunfermline Athletic (League Cup) on 22nd August, 2006.

Even allowing for the limited importance of the Irn Bru Cup it could not be denied that successive defeats highlighted a concern ahead of

the forthcoming top of the table clash away to Raith Rovers. The concern mounted with the news that Ross Docherty, Craig Moore, Paddy Boyle and Jamie Adams were definitely ruled out by injury. To worsen this situation there were doubts about the availability of Alan Forrest, Robbie Crawford and Andy Geggan. Only Andy Geggan of the three made it into the squad and he succeeded in playing for the entire match.

A new signing went straight into the team. This was striker Lawrence Shankland who had played for Scotland at under-21 level and who, in the previous season, had played against Ayr United for St.Mirren and Morton. The date of his Ayr debut was 9th September so he had not had the benefit of pre-season training. In light of his imminent form it can only be concluded that clubs made a large oversight by leaving him unattached in the summer. He was to become the first ever Ayr United player to score in his first four competitive matches for the club. The nearest contender was Charlie Howe who had scored in the first three league fixtures of the club's history back in 1910. Shankland's first goal in an Ayr United shirt came in the second minute of the second half. Even this early in the season it was reasonable to view the Raith Rovers fixture as a six-pointer. Three minutes later Lewis Vaughan equalised from a free-kick. After nine more minutes had elapsed Jason Thomson put the home team ahead with a weak shot. The two conceded goals were avoidable and might simply have been defined as calamitous. Pressure mounted to get level but the match petered out into a 2-1 defeat and a highly dubious red card for Chris Higgins. We remained in second place but the gap was now four points.

In looking to remain in contention there was little margin for error as we contemplated a visit from Alloa Athletic, a club that would prove hugely influential in the quest for promotion in general and the title in particular. Former Ayr United players in their starting line-up were Scott Taggart, Daryll Meggatt and Kevin Cawley. Another, Craig Malcolm, would join the fray as a substitute. Andy Graham is well remembered for his role in hitting the decisive kick in our shootout against Stranraer in the 2016 play-off final and he too would have been an ex-Ayr player in the visiting line-up had it not been for injury. With six minutes remaining and the score tied at 2-2 a penalty was awarded for a supposed handling offence by Jamie Adams. Scott Taggart scored from the spot and we only salvaged a 3-3 draw when

Lawrence Shankland got his second goal of the match in the fourth minute of stoppage time. Film evidence proved that the penalty kick was awarded wrongly. On the Monday Ian McCall got a telephone call of apology from referee Euan Anderson. This was a decent gesture but a little disheartening.

For the second consecutive Saturday a winning performance had failed to produce a win. In particular the match at Kirkcaldy had the fans streaming from the ground in a state of bewilderment. In calm reflection some proffered the view that luck will even itself out over the course of the season. Credence was given to that view at Hampden when Queen's Park's David Galt struck a shot that hit the inside of Jordan Hart's post and the ball came out. With just five minutes played we could reflect on a lucky break. On another day it might have rebounded in. Ten minutes into the second half, while leading by a Jamie Adams goal, there was an 'oh no!' moment when a penalty was awarded for a Michael Rose challenge on Luke Donnelly. The sense of foreboding was relieved when Jordan Hart saved the spot kick from Ross Millen then Luke Donnelly's shot from the rebound. Lawrence Shankland settled it at 2-0 with a goal against one of his former clubs.

We still trailed Raith Rovers by six points and there was a feeling that we had to exercise patience in the hope that they would experience a slip-up. It happened! Albion Rovers 2 Raith Rovers 1 assumed almost as much importance as Ayr United 3 East Fife 0. Albion Rovers could now be seen as a threat since they sat in third place and our lead over them was merely one point. Yet this was as good as it got for them since they stood to be condemned to bottom place on the final day.

Missed chances were rued in a 2-2 draw at home to Airdrie and with Raith Rovers winning 2-0 at home to Arbroath they established a gap of five points. One week later the Stranraer versus Raith Rovers match was abandoned when the pitch got waterlogged. Ayr United extracted the fullest advantage with a 5-0 win at Forfar which featured a Michael Moffat hat-trick. It was the third time we had won at Station Park by this precise scoreline each time being in a league fixture. New Year's Day 1937 may have been outwith living memory but your writer can recall having a conversation with Archie Scott in which he recalled going to that match in a chartered train. Some of you may remember Archie in his capacity of travel convenor of the Ayr United Supporters' Association. Within living memory was our second 5-0 win at Forfar on 9th February, 1985, when the match was played in blizzard conditions. Reminiscing can be a pleasant pastime but it was even more pleasant to take stock of the situation here in 2017. The gap was now two points, albeit that we had played a game more.

Forfar Athletic recovered from being routed by securing a 1-1 draw at home to Raith Rovers in their next match. Ayr United 2 Stranraer 0 ended in the team in elusive pursuit of a third goal which would have meant regaining top place on goal difference. The season continued to be a statistical heaven. Fifty-two competitive goals had been scored by the end of October. It was only our third season ever in which the fifty-goal barrier had been breached by this point of the season. It had happened in 1957/58 with fifty-five and 1958/59 with fifty-four. Steven Bell was one of the two Stranraer players red-carded on that afternoon but he would conclude the season with happier recollections of Somerset Park when receiving the League One trophy as Ayr United captain. Mention of this links seamlessly to another statistic. The largest number of Ayr United captains in a season is four. Successive injuries in season 2017/18 meant that the captaincy began with Ross Docherty then passed in turn to Chris Higgins, Paddy Boyle and Steven Bell.

The prospect of going to Arbroath was fraught with danger in the context of the home team having beaten Airdrie 7-1 in their previous home game. It transpired that there was nothing to fear. A 4-1 win included three goals in a five-minute burst and the two goals from Lawrence Shankland took his total to nine in the eight games in which he had donned an Ayr United shirt. Raith Rovers also won on that afternoon but it was a more miserly 1-0 at home to East Fife. We had now regained top place on goal difference but with an extra game played. With the clubs scheduled to meet in the next fixture there was a degree of excitement.

Irritatingly our opponents had to fulfil an Irn Bru Cup quarter-final at Dumbarton on the scheduled Saturday but the hotly anticipated meeting was deferred merely to the Tuesday night. Lawrence Shankland and Robbie Crawford made it 2-0 by the midway point of the first half and Craig Moore sealed a 3-0 victory in the last action of the match. It was even possible to afford the luxury of a missed penalty. Our total of league goals for the season was now thirty-eight. This was the highest in the British Leagues albeit shared with Manchester City.

The opportunity to immediately kick on was denied by the intervention of the Scottish Cup. Banks O' Dee at Spain Park in

Aberdeen was truly a trip into the unknown, although there was a warning sign when that club won 10-0 on the Saturday before. Aberdeenshire Juniors versus League One. Even in acknowledging the undisputed fact that the home team excelled at their own level surely there was no danger. Lawrence Shankland scored in thirty-two seconds to create a club record for the quickest Scottish Cup goal. Two penalties were conceded both of which were converted and at 2-1 down there was potential for embarrassment. By half-time we had a 4-2 lead which was extended to 6-2 by the close. In time for the next match it was announced that Lawrence Shankland had agreed to extend his short-term deal until the end of the season.

When Craig Moore struck the decisive goal in a 2-1 win at Alloa the game had reached stoppage time. Even when the going got tough this team had the propensity to keep on winning. Assuredly the going was liable to be tough even in the face of supposedly inferior opposition. It is an easy trait to look down a fixture list and to make a mental note of games which seem almost certain to be won. On the first two Saturdays of December 2017 Albion Rovers then Queen's Park were at Ayr. It was difficult not to fall for the assumption that six points would be taken. Against Albion Rovers it was 1-1 at an uncomfortably late stage. Then, in the 73rd minute, Declan McDaid cut the ball back for Lawrence Shankland to fire the team ahead. The relief was merely temporary. Two minutes later our former player Alan Trouten made it 2-2. The wait for the next goal was also two minutes and it was a Chris Higgins header which enabled a 3-2 victory. Taking the points for granted may have been a foolhardy notion and, although all three points were taken, it was a somewhat tortuous process.

Ayr United versus Queen's Park was top versus bottom and the thoughts of the fans again drifted towards the notion of a straightforward win with the potential to boost the goal difference. In the 24th minute Lewis Magee brought down Lawrence Shankland for a penalty kick from which Craig Moore scored. Three minutes before half-time Conor McVey levelled it and three minutes beyond half-time Craig Reid had the misfortune to slice a clearance into his own net. 2-1 down at home to the bottom club! Declan McDaid (79) and Alan Forrest (88) turned it around for a 3-2 win but there was a dawning realisation that acquiring the points was a tough process.

Away to East Fife the trend of awkward opposition reared its head again. Inside the first ten minutes Kevin Smith shot against

Jordan Hart's crossbar from ten yards and Jonathan Page contrived to head the rebound over. With the home side having the better of the exchanges it was a disappointment rather than a shock when Chris Duggan fired the homesters ahead in the 36th minute. When the half-time whistle was blown our 1-0 deficit was an understated reflection of the course of the match. His team may have been outplayed so far but Ian McCall had faith in his players' tenacity. Michael Rose equalised then put the team in front. Craig Moore and Lawrence Shankland then applied the shine to a result which read East Fife 1 Ayr United 4. After the match Mr McCall said: "I can't remember a squad that has scored so many goals. Our players are so clinical and they never give up."

Nine consecutive wins had now been recorded. This comprised eight league fixtures and one Scottish Cup tie. It comprised a club best since the run of ten wins between 23rd November, 1968, and 1st February, 1969 (nine in the league and one in the Scottish Cup). A win at Airdrie was now required to equal the feat achieved in 1968/69 and then the onus would be on chasing the club record of twelve consecutive wins between 24th October, 1936, and 2nd January, 1937, all of which were in the league. Airdrie 2 Ayr United 0 – at least there was the considerable consolation of having witnessed the third longest run of wins in our history. This match against Airdrie and the Hibs League Cup tie would be the only two matches in which Ayr United would fail to score in all season. It was a feat which comprised a club record albeit shared with 1936/37. From these statistics you will have deduced that no visiting team left Somerset Park with a clean sheet in the whole of 2017/18.

For the second time in December we took part in a top versus bottom fixture, Forfar Athletic having taken over the basement position from Queen's Park. At 2-0 up with fifteen minutes remaining the proceedings were in line with expectation. Ayr United 2 Forfar Athletic 3 – with goals timed at 75, 83 and 88 it was lost in a pantomime of calamitous defending. Before this match Forfar Athletic had played forty-seven league games at Ayr and the breakdown included thirty-three Ayr United wins and eight draws. They also came to Ayr with selection difficulties and memories of a 5-0 defeat when the teams had met in October. Quite naturally there were grumblings but the root cause was slackness rather than complacency.

A fixture at Stranraer on Tuesday, 2nd January, afforded an immediate chance to atone. The chance was taken. It was 5-0 by the 63rd minute and 5-1 at the end. This equalled our largest margin of league victory at Stair Park (shared with an identical result on 26th March, 1966). It was also our biggest margin of league victory at the start of a year since beating Berwick Rangers 4-0 at Ayr on 2nd January, 2008, and our biggest margin of away victory at the start of a year since Morton 0 Ayr United 6 on 2nd January, 2001. Some readers will be able to recall a 7-1 win at Stranraer on 16th February, 1974, but that was, of course, in the Scottish Cup. This win in 2018 broke a sequence whereby we had lost our first game of the year in the previous six years. In returning from this statistical digression you may be told that Stranraer captain Steven Bell was signed on an eighteen-month deal three days later. He said: "I couldn't knock back the chance to come to Ayr once the manager made his interest known."

On the evening of 2nd January the top of the table indicated that title success was very much in the balance.

	P	W	D	L	F	A	Points
Ayr United	20	14	2	4	57	26	44
Raith Rovers	18	13	3	2	40	15	42
Alloa Athletic	18	8	4	6	28	23	28

It was a bleak process to view the list of longer-term injury victims together with those added more recently. Out of contention to play against Arbroath were Michael Rose, Brian Gilmour, Craig McGuffie, Andy Geggan, Robbie Crawford and Ross Docherty. With the match underway the situation worsened. In the 57th minute Chris Higgins got stretchered off and his season was over. By that time we had a 1-0 lead by courtesy of an Alan Forrest goal in the opening minutes. Seven days earlier the fans had gazed across Somerset Park in virtual disbelief at a capitulation against Forfar. With the steps retraced we had once more to look on in almost equal disbelief as the game took on similar developments. Ryan Wallace punished indecisive defending by ramming home the equaliser from close range in the 68th minute. When Thomas O'Brien got sent off in the 81st minute the advantage just had to be with the eleven full-timers rather than the ten part-timers. Against Forfar the losing goal was conceded in the 88th minute and it was to happen again. Jordan Hart advanced from his goal to make an interception but succeeded only in making a fresh-air kick while stranded. Leighton McIntosh then availed himself of the opportunity to deposit the ball in the vacant net. Ayr United 1 Arbroath 2 – the result was as warmly received in Kirkcaldy as it was in Arbroath.

There is a faction of any team's support who subscribe to the view that there is no point in being concerned about matches happening elsewhere but, as season 2017/18 progressed, it was clear that we did have a vested interest in what Raith Rovers were doing. On exiting disconsolately after the Arbroath defeat you can be assured that the depression deepened a little more on being appraised of the news that Raith Rovers had beaten Forfar Athletic at Stark's Park.

The league table was an illustration of several grounds for worry. We were now one point off the top having played two games more. In playing out a 'what if?' scenario there was the obvious conclusion that Raith Rovers, by virtue of their games in hand, had the potential to stretch their lead to seven points and with the teams due to play each other at Kirkcaldy in the next match they even had the potential for a ten-point lead. In calm reflection a different picture was painted in the mind. There was no guarantee that our adversaries would win their games in hand and, in the event of beating them, we would be back on top.

Two days before the big match goalkeeper Jack Ruddy was fixed up on loan from Wolves. He was a Scotland under-21 internationalist and at 6'5" he had a very commanding presence. Our new man went straight into the starting-line-up. The importance of the occasion was not lost on an Ayr team that looked high on motivation. An adverse consequence of this gut determination was a yellow card count of six. It meant that Craig Reid, Paddy Boyle, Jamie Adams, Craig Moore, Steven Bell and Michael Moffat had all to cautiously guard against a second misdemeanour. The Raith Rovers team was a bit more restrained with just one (for Euan Murray). Eleven minutes before half-time a beautifully worked move was finished off by Lawrence Shankland who skilfully lobbed the ball beyond Graeme Smith, the advancing goalkeeper. Seven minutes later Iain Davidson brought down Lawrence Shankland for what looked like a clear penalty. Referee Barry Cook viewed it differently. Two minutes into the second half Lewis Vaughan struck a free-kick across the face of the Ayr goal and Greig Spence was able to shoot the equalising goal. The implications of defeat would have been grave but a 1-1 draw was played out in a predominantly fast-paced, ill-tempered and tense manner.

The last home match had been against Arbroath and so was the next one. Arbroath had won their two league fixtures at Ayr thus far in the season so they must have considered this Scottish Cup fourth round tie to be winnable. Their Scottish Cup record against Ayr United was impeccable. The clubs had only met once previously in the competition and that was on 27th January, 1968, when they had won 2-0 at Ayr. Some of us could recall watching that tie of a half-century earlier and there was repayment in full in 2018. Ayr United 4 Arbroath 1 – the major post match publicity was about Arbroath manager Dick Campbell taking to the pitch to confront the referee about the non-award of a penalty kick. With one match still left in January our goals count in all competitions was highly impressive at ninety.

A half-time lead of 2-0 at Hampden may have looked comfortable to anyone not at the match and simply checking score updates. Craig Moore had scored after five minutes and then Queen's Park took the initiative by gaining the most possession. Alan Forrest's goal two minutes from the interval was a great relief in a match that was proving tricky. Queen's Park entered the match as the second bottom club and by the close of play they would be at the foot. Yet their league plight was in contradiction to a style of play which saw them consistently attack in waves. By the midway point of the second half it was becoming an uncomfortable spectacle. In the 76th minute Craig McGuffie was sent on and four minutes later he scored with a nicely measured curling shot. The game had turned. With three minutes left he scored a replica of his first goal and it was gratifying to see the 4-0 scoreline on Hampden's illuminated scoreboard. There was still time for Adam Cummins to narrow the deficit with a header from a corner-kick but a 4-1 win was enough cause for the fans to celebrate by singing on the way out of the ground. It was known that the Raith Rovers game at Alloa was scoreless therefore the top place had been regained by a point but it had to be acknowledged that we had played a game more. Mark Kerr made his Ayr United debut in this match against Queen's Park. He had worked with Ian McCall at Falkirk and Dundee United and the deal was until the end of the season.

The influence of Alloa Athletic on the outcome of League One in 2017/18 has already been acknowledged and that influence was to intensify in the last days of the campaign. On the first Saturday in February, Lawrence Shankland scored in the 10th minute at home to Alloa. Four minutes later Jamie McCart punished static defending

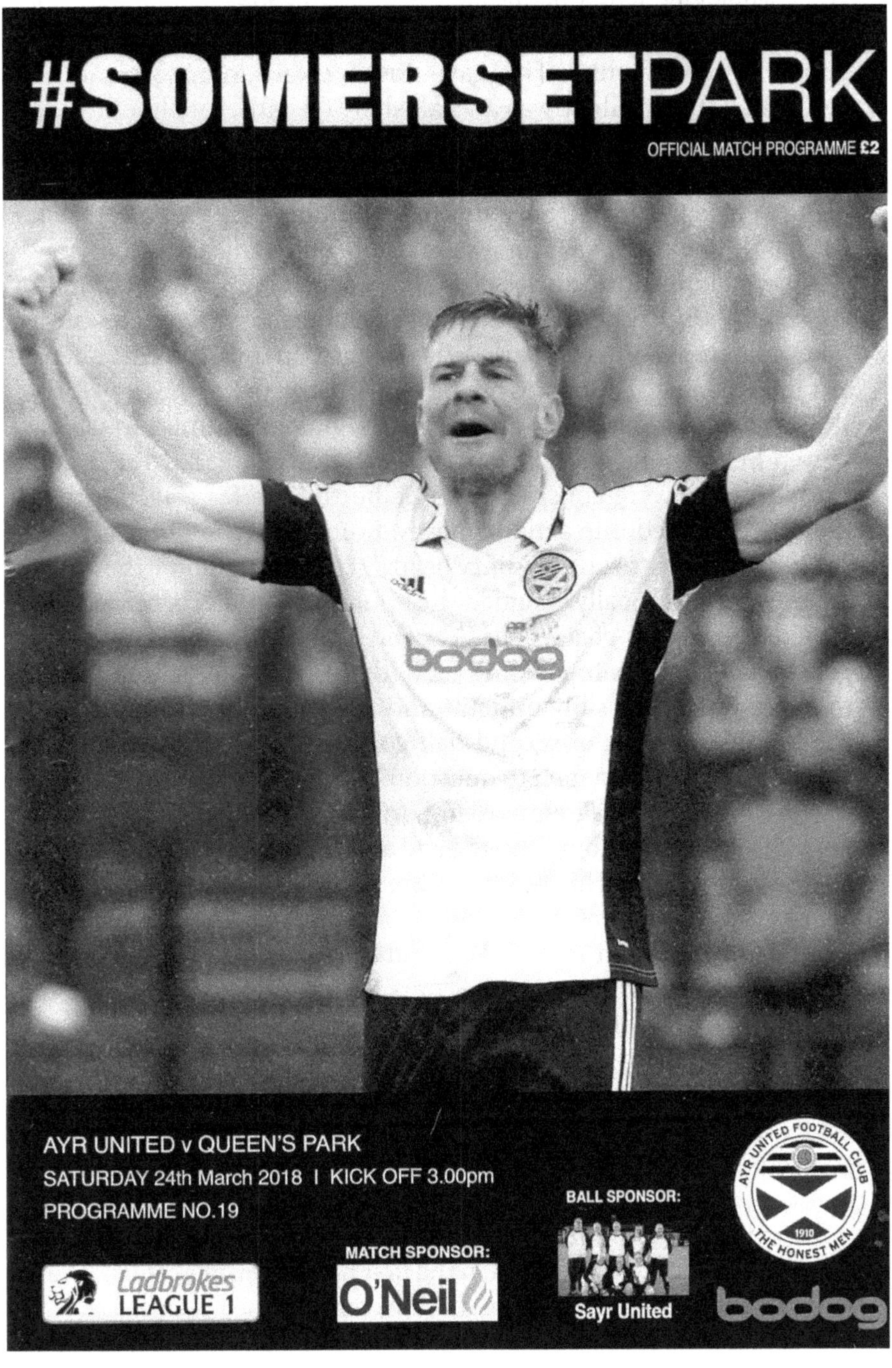

#SOMERSETPARK

OFFICIAL MATCH PROGRAMME £2

AYR UNITED v QUEEN'S PARK
SATURDAY 24th March 2018 I KICK OFF 3.00pm
PROGRAMME NO.19

BALL SPONSOR:

MATCH SPONSOR:
O'Neil

Sayr United

bodog

at a corner-kick when he levelled it with a header. Barely had the discontent subsided when Jack Ruddy miskicked a ball that was bouncing towards him. This gave Ross Stewart an opportunity to get in a shot. Luckily it was a weak shot. Or rather it should have been lucky. Ruddy attempted to track back in order to make a save but he was thwarted when he slipped. Agonisingly the ball ended up being lodged in the net. Seventy-three minutes were left to get back level. It did not happen. The season had been handicapped by some chequered home form and the top spot was relinquished once more.

Scottish Cup time brought the season's second live television broadcast from Somerset Park. With Rangers in town a media circus was unavoidable. The names on the injury list were Robbie Crawford, Ross Docherty, Mark Kerr and Chris Higgins in addition to which Steven Bell was ineligible through being cup-tied. Paddy Boyle and Andy Geggan were considered to be borderline for selection but they were pressed into action anyway. Even Ian McCall himself was a casualty. Owing to an eye injury he had to remain at home therefore his assistant Neil Scally assumed the role as boss. Alan Forrest scored by sliding in when goalkeeper Wes Foderingham was struggling to get control of the ball. Holding on to that 1-0 lead for seventy-nine minutes was impossibly difficult and the eventual 6-1 defeat was attributable to a run of second half goals during a phase when the sense of urgency was open to question.

Ayr United 3 East Fife 0 – Alan Forrest got the third goal from a penalty kick half an hour from the end and it was our 99th competitive goal of the season. This rendered the crowd interest emphatically alive as the century was desperately anticipated. It would be deferred merely until the next match. The shutout against East Fife was our first since the 3-0 win over Raith Rovers back on 14th November. There was a bonus too. Albion Rovers 2 Raith Rovers 2 – Alan Trouten had converted a penalty in the third minute of stoppage time to ensure that just one point would be going back to Kirkcaldy. On taking stock we were now six points off the top with a game in hand, a superior goal difference and the knowledge that Raith Rovers had still to come to Ayr.

To whom would fall the honour of the 100th goal? The Airdrie defence could not be breached in the first half but Somerset Park was lit up by the landmark goal five minutes beyond the break. A Declan McDaid corner-kick was not cleared effectively and the ball landed for Mark Kerr who transferred it back to McDaid. It was crossed again only for it to strike defender Dean Cairns on the back. It then broke neatly for Andy Geggan to strike it into the net. The same player who had scored number one back in July had the honour of hitting number 100 here in February. Lawrence Shankland made it 2-0 from a penalty and then tied it up at 3-0, both of his goals coming in the last ten minutes. 3-0 wins at home on consecutive Saturdays – in the process Ayr United became the first team in the British leagues to hit a century of competitive goals in 2017/18. While basking in the glory of 102 goals news emerged that Arbroath had scored in the 89th minute to gain a 2-2 draw against Raith Rovers at Stark's Park. We were now just four points off the top with a game in hand.

This was only the seventh time an Ayr United team had exceeded one hundred goals in a season. The other seasons were 1927/28, 1936/37, 1955/56, 1957/58, 1958/59 and 1987/88.

Weather conditions stalled the assault on the title. On Saturday, 3rd March, conditions knocked out our match at Arbroath and the Raith Rovers match at Forfar. The Raith Rovers fixture was quickly rescheduled to the immediate Tuesday only to suffer another postponement and on the same night Albion Rovers versus Ayr United befell the same fate. The weather Gods had conspired nicely. It all meant that the next fixture was Raith Rovers at home and, with the top of the table looking like this, it was intriguing even to neutrals.

	P	W	D	L	F	A	Points
Raith Rovers	27	17	7	3	55	25	58
Ayr United	26	17	3	6	70	32	54

Neither team was in the mood to ease gently into it. There was little in the way of tentative exchanges. From the beginning the pace was fast and it was altogether intense. It was combative in a way that befitted just how important the occasion was. Something just had to give and, when it did, it happened at the Somerset Road end. Declan McDaid delivered a free-kick into the box and it was met by the head of Lawrence Shankland then firmly planted in the net. It was the 34th minute and the reaction was frenzied. Two minutes before half-time Kyle Benedictus misheaded the ball in the direction of Jamie Adams, whose shot lacked power but nonetheless slipped through the grasp of goalkeeper Aaron Lennox for 2-0. When Michael Moffat made it 3-0 eight minutes after the interval some visiting fans were seen to leave the ground. There was a total ruthlessness about the performance and we had consecutive 3-0 win number three. The ramifications of it all were huge. Ayr United now sat one point off the top with a game in hand and a superior goal difference. Quite apart from every other positive connotation it was a big psychological victory.

Too many games were left for complacency, yet the feelings of elation could not be stifled. One point off the top with a game less played amounted to pole position though and there was a hope that the defeat of our rivals at Ayr was the preliminary for a run of adverse form from them. Forfar Athletic 2 Raith Rovers 1 – on the immediate Tuesday it seemed possible that such hope would materialise. Straight away there was a chance to regain the top spot. That opportunity was afforded by our match at Arbroath on the next night. Gayfield Park has an unfortunate location. It juts out into the North Sea and it is therefore prone to windy conditions. Ayr United first played at that location on 2nd January, 1926, and in the intervening years our match reports from that ground have often contained references to the wind. Some of you may even remember Michael Donald getting soaked by a wave which came over the sea wall. On the night of 14th March, 2018, the wind was bad, even by the standards of Arbroath. The conditions gave the illusion that they were playing with a beach ball. Arbroath had wind advantage in the first half and as the game approached half-time it was scoreless. This was ideal. However the idyll was spoiled when Danny Denholm put the ball in the Ayr net in the final minute of the first half. The perceived second-half advantage was not entirely straightforward. Crossfield passing was rendered difficult by the wind's swirling nature and the tendency to overhit had also to be curbed. Thirteen minutes from the end Craig McGuffie was sent on, and if ever a game was crying out for a player with skill this was it. Four minutes from the end he played a one-two with Steven Bell then got in behind the Arbroath defence to score from a narrow angle. Then, in the 88th minute, Lawrence Shankland shot against a post. At 1-1 it was enough to hit the top on goal difference and with a game in hand.

We returned to the same district on the Saturday to play Forfar Athletic. A 5-0 win on our previous visit could now be dismissed as irrelevant. They had since won at Ayr and more recently been victorious over Raith Rovers. Conditions at Station Park were windy although it was nowhere near as bad as the Arbroath experience. As the match entered the last ten minutes we only had a Michael Moffat goal to show for a lot of attacking momentum. Then a Craig Moore penalty kick settled any lingering uncertainty at 2-0. Raith Rovers versus East Fife was scheduled for the Sunday in order that it could be screened live on BBC Alba. With a vested interest in the result you can be sure that it would have had decent viewing figures in Ayr and district had it not been for a postponement due to icy conditions and a snow-covered pitch.

In theory the task was now simple. That task was to nail the league title and kill off the challenge from our counterparts in Fife. In practice the task was far from simple. The action now switched to Coatbridge on a Tuesday night and with Albion Rovers desperately fighting to avoid the drop there was never going to be much likelihood that they would be steamrolled. Craig Moore (28) and Jamie Adams (36) – 2-0 up! It was not outrageously optimistic to believe that it was just a matter of time before being crowned champions. Kane Hester (39) and Alan Trouten (66) – 2-2! Lawrence Shankland (75) – 3-2 winners! The road to the title was a rocky one. As if to emphasise that last statement Albion Rovers had a penalty claim in the final minute. Sean Higgins went down under a challenge from Andy Geggan. To huge relief referee Finnie paid no heed.

Constant reappraisal of the top placings amounted to a perfectly natural exercise. When the final whistle pierced the night air in Coatbridge our lead amounted to six points and we had a far better goal difference but we had played one game more. With the score sitting at Lawrence Shankland 3 Queen's Park 0 (not a typo!) after thirty-four minutes the position was further consolidated. His hat-trick put victory beyond doubt. At the time of writing Ayr United remain in the situation of never having lost a league fixture in which the team has acquired a 3-0 half-time lead. The only match the club has ever lost from this position was a Scottish Cup tie at Inverness on 27th January, 2001. A Craig Moore penalty kick boosted it to 4-0. There was some expectation and even more hope that Raith Rovers would falter at Airdrie on that afternoon. As if to keep the tension alive they won 2-1.

The comprehensive result against Queen's Park was merely a temporary reprieve. Once more we were thrust into the domain of difficult matches against stubborn opposition. Alan Forrest seized onto a long ball from Lawrence Shankland then turned inside to fire Ayr United into a fourth minute lead against East Fife but the home team refused to be easily suppressed. Chris Duggan (22 and 53) overturned the scoreline in favour of the Fifers to cause more delight eleven miles away at Stark's Park than right there at the Bayview Stadium. Steven Bell (72) headed home a Craig McGuffie corner-kick from six yards. Would the desperately sought winner happen? With two minutes of regulation time left Craig Watson put in a coarse challenge on Steven Bell. Penalty! Craig Moore had the fans in raptures when he converted it. At the point of going 3-2 up at Methil the Raith Rovers versus Albion Rovers match, which was running several minutes behind, remained scoreless. For it to remain scoreless for the last few minutes was seemingly too much to hope for. The Albion Rovers defence was breached twice in the last four minutes so it was a 2-0 home win. Four games to go! A three-point lead! A greatly superior goal difference!

Back on the road again the destination was Airdrie. A significant change involved a recall for Jordan Hart to replace Jack Ruddy in goal. With ten minutes on the clock Dale Carrick nodded Airdrie in front. Although discomforting, it was known that this Ayr team had the physical and mental capacity to hit back. Robbie Crawford (37) and Lawrence Shankland (70) proved this point in a 2-1 win. Paddy Boyle had to go off nine minutes from the end. With an arm in plaster his season was over. The march of time would prove that his Ayr United career was now over. Arbroath 1 Raith Rovers 1 – only the most partisan fans of Raith Rovers held out even the slightest notion that their team still had a chance of winning the league. With three fixtures left the top of the table had a majestic look.

	P	W	D	L	F	A	Points
Ayr United	33	23	4	6	88	38	73
Raith Rovers	33	20	8	5	63	32	68

Two of the remaining fixtures were at home and even if it did come down to goal difference the league trophy would still be coming to Ayr. What could possibly go wrong? That question will now be addressed.

On 14th April it was possible, but unlikely, that the title could be clinched. The attendance at the Ayr United versus Stranraer fixture was 2,323. With a greater certainty of becoming champions on this day the attendance would have been in the region of double that. It was expected that Stranraer would be beaten in which case the title would be ours if Raith Rovers versus Queen's Park ended in a draw or an away win. The assumption was that it would end in a home win and it did (2-0). It was envisaged that we would take care of Stranraer then head to Alloa for the second last game requiring just a draw to win the league.

Let us now digress back from what was imagined to what actually happened. To use that old greyhound analogy Stranraer came flying out of the traps. In just the third minute Grant Anderson scored with a looping header. The last two matches had seen Ayr United come from behind to win and there was no shortage of time to pull it off again. However there was a sense that it was going to be more difficult this time. The Stranraer team looked high on incentive and there was no inkling that any quarter would be conceded. In the 16th minute though an equaliser did happen when Jamie Adams scored with a header from a corner-kick. Maybe, just maybe, the early indications had given a false impression of the eventual outcome. Or maybe not! In the 32nd minute Lawrence Shankland got red-carded for the alleged use of an elbow on Morgyn Neill. There was a collective groan around the ground when the red card was hoisted. It was potentially fatal to our chances not only of winning the match but the title too. His goals count sat at twenty-nine for the season, including three in the Scottish Cup. It was known that he would be suspended for the final two matches. He looked crestfallen when leaving the pitch. In the 85th minute Kyle Turner went down under a challenge from Jamie Adams and a penalty was awarded. Scott Agnew scored and at 2-1 down there was no comeback. Was Lawrence Shankland vilified by the fans for his red card and the prospective repercussions? The opposite was true. He virtually swept the boards at that evening's Player of The Year event, and his name was repeatedly sung with enough volume to disturb the sparrows in the rafters. Ian McCall said that of all the clubs he had been at he had never known a player to have such a high level of adulation. There was, however, a lingering fear that one of his suitors would make a move for him on the imminent expiry of his contract. On the day when he scored a hat-trick against Queen's Park prominent spectators were Hearts manager Craig Levein and Graeme Mathie, the head of recruitment at Hibs.

With two games left our leading margin was now down to a nerve-inducing two points. Working on the assumption that Raith

Rovers would win their last two games we now required four points. Yet, in view of the next round of fixtures, it was maybe wrong to blindly accept that they would mop up the final six points. On the penultimate weekend these were the vital matches.

>Stranraer versus Raith Rovers (Saturday).
>Alloa Athletic versus Ayr United (Sunday).

Stranraer had performed most impressively at Ayr. This was a team that looked capable of beating Raith Rovers seven days later. The Ayr United game was moved to the Sunday in order that it could be broadcast live on television by BBC Alba. With a Stranraer win on the Saturday then the minimum of a draw at Alloa a day later we would be guaranteed to finish top. Prior to the unexpected Stranraer defeat there had been a strong feeling that it was going to be resolved in our favour at Alloa. This prompted people to reminisce about having been there in 1988 when the title was won. The score updates from Stranraer were soon to remove thoughts of a repeat at Alloa in 2018. With just five minutes played the home team went a goal down and the final damage was 3-0. A lead that had seemed uncatchable had now been caught. We were now overtaken at the top by a point. Two games were left in comparison to their one. At the very least it was essential not to lose on the Sunday. Either way our target remained at four points.

Your writer likes the town of Alloa. As well as having worked in the area it is a place that appears in my family history. My great-grandparents got married there on 25th May, 1880, at which time my great-granny stayed at the workers' houses at the Alloa glassworks, but on 22nd April, 2018, family history was a considerably more distant notion than the immediate future of Ayr United Football Club. The Ayr support was 1,162 in the overall crowd of 1,749. This was outstanding when it was considered that it was live on television and nothing would be decided on the day anyway. Immediately after kick-off a definite tension hung in the air. In the 21st minute that tension was transformed into depression when Kevin Cawley played in Iain Flannigan who struck the ball beyond Jordan Hart for the opening goal. Twelve minutes later Callum Crane fired home another for 2-0 and the depression deepened within the ground but to the television public in Kirkcaldy these scenes caused great joy. It was an illustration of the 'them or us' syndrome. Them or us? Right then you would have been more likely to back them for the league. At the start of the second half there was clearly a positive reaction to what had been said at half-time. Heavy pressure quickly mounted on Neil Parry's goal and it paid a handsome dividend five minutes after the restart. Craig McGuffie made a good run then laid the ball off to Craig Moore who rounded the goalkeeper and got a scoring shot away just before the angle threatened to get too acute. The fans went wild. At 2-1 there was the thought that even a draw would put us in control of our own destiny. In the 78th minute Callum Smith pushed David Ferguson. Penalty to Ayr! In a manner of speaking we were back in control. Sink the penalty then win next Saturday and we would be champions! Your writer's stance was behind the goal thus affording a close view of Craig Moore hitting the ball over the crossbar and off into the direction of the Ochil Hills. The disappointment was deep yet there was nothing in the way of criticism for a player who would end the season with more goals than starting appearances. It was reminiscent of the Lawrence Shankland red card. How could you possibly direct criticism at players who had produced consistently excellent performances? The twelve remaining minutes were badly frustrating and the outlook, as you will see here, seemed dire.

	P	W	D	L	F	A	Points
Raith Rovers	35	22	8	5	68	32	74
Ayr United	35	23	4	8	90	42	73

The last day fixtures were:

Ayr United versus Albion Rovers.
Raith Rovers versus Alloa Athletic.

With three games left our lead was five points and with one game left we had to survey this. It was already confirmed that Alloa would be in the play-offs and there was a school of thought that they would be taking it easy in preparation for their exertions in the midweek ahead. After our defeat at Alloa I got talking to one of their fans in the town. He was introduced as "old John" and then it came out in conversation that I was older than him by three days! Anyway he said that there was nothing to worry about. He was adamant that his team would win at Kirkcaldy. Raith Rovers were unbeaten at home in the league all season. It was also a reminder of boasts from Stranraer that they would beat Raith Rovers after winning at Ayr. Even a draw for Alloa would suffice provided, of course, that we could see off Albion Rovers. Balanced against just how much was at stake for Raith Rovers it was considered that they would get the win that would take them over the line.

It was reminiscent of 2008/09 when the clubs were neck and neck in the closing weeks and they won the Second Division title on beating Queen's Park at Hampden in the second-last match. Their success happened because of our failure to beat Alloa Athletic at Somerset Park on the same afternoon. It was further reminiscent of 1986/87 when we required a last day draw at home to Stirling Albion for promotion. The match was lost and there was an unexpected promotion for Raith Rovers (along with champions Meadowbank Thistle) on account of their win at Stranraer. Another 'them or us' scenario happened on the last day of season 1983/84. We had to win at Dumbarton to avoid relegation, this task being made more difficult by the home team being so strong that they were already guaranteed promotion to the Premier League. On the assumption that relegation rivals Raith Rovers would win away to Meadowbank Thistle (they did!) even a draw at Boghead Park would have consigned Ayr United to the drop along with the already doomed Alloa Athletic. Dumbarton 0 Ayr United 3 was the scarcely believable outcome. Vying with Raith Rovers can be traced back for a considerable length of time. On 4th April, 1908, Ayr FC played East Stirling at Somerset Park in the Second Division's final league fixture. An Ayr FC win was required to put the club one point ahead of top-placed Dumbarton who had completed all their fixtures. The East Stirling match ended 1-1 so Dumbarton remained top on goal average. Third-placed Raith Rovers had two games still to play and they sat one point behind the joint leaders. They won them both to come from behind to win the league by a three-point margin.

On the morning of 28th April, 2018, it is doubtful whether any Ayr United supporters were thinking too distantly into the past although it is possible that minds may have been occupied by what might have been at Alloa or in the home game against Stranraer the week before that. As kick-off time approached there was a cocktail of emotions. Had we blown it or was it going to be gloriously snatched back? The attendance was 2,441. This figure was consistent with the uncertainty. Had our fate been in our own hands the crowd figure might reasonably have been double. Over at Stark's Park an attendance of 4,496 mirrored the expectation there.

No matter how long someone supports Ayr United it is not possible to get conditioned to frights. Indeed it was a most definite fright when Sean Higgins of Albion Rovers sent the ball across the face of the Ayr goal and it was met by Michael Mullin who contrived to send it high and wide from a very short range. In the 34th minute Declan McDaid took a corner-kick on the right. It fell for Jamie Adams who headed it on. Goalkeeper Kieran Wright palmed it away but Craig Moore was there to touch it over the line for 1-0. Between then and half-time extreme rain showers fell, but outside of the game in progress all that concerned anyone was that the Raith Rovers game was still scoreless. For what it was worth Ayr United were back on top of the league at half-time. When the second half kicked-off we face an unanticipated complication. Queen's Park were unexpectedly beating Arbroath at Hampden. This meant that Albion Rovers had dropped into bottom place. A win for Queen's Park (it happened) would mean that the team we were facing at Ayr would require a draw in order to get the second bottom position which would give them a chance of survival via the play-offs. The additional incentive was evident and there would be a vulnerability for as long as it stayed at 1-0. Constantly the fans busily checked score updates. So far so good! Four minutes from the end Michael Moffat made ground down the right then sent the ball across the face of goal. Declan McDaid then succeeded in holding off the attention of Conor Scullion to drive it home for 2-0. In time-honoured fashion the fans received the goal with the traditional expressions of delight but, even although the game was as good as won, there was a hint of restraint due to the very large elephant in the room. What was the Raith score? 0-0. Seconds then minutes later it was still 0-0.

Then came what surely must be a contender for the oddest episode witnessed at Somerset Park since the ground was opened in 1888. The final whistle blew on Ayr United 2 Albion Rovers 0. Nobody drifted towards the exits. Even the visiting fans stayed back to applaud their team's valiant efforts. Out on the field the Ayr United players stood around either on their own or in small groups. Some looked as if they were praying and there was some shrugging of the shoulders. The

Raith Rovers game was still in progress. We needed it to finish fast and we needed it to stay at 0-0. In the Stand and on the terraces the wonder of modern technology allowed the supporters to keep refreshing score updates. It would be a gross understatement to suggest that these were worrying minutes. The wait was simply terror stricken. How long was this going to last? A spontaneous roar broke the silence and it came from the Stand. The clamour quickly spread to other parts of the ground and there was an immediate pitch invasion. Players jumped around in sheer delight. When the initial roar went up I refreshed Livescore on my phone and it was not showing the Raith Rovers game as having reached full time. I refreshed it again and there was the telltale FT in all of its glory. It was a fantastic feeling to join in the celebrations albeit that I was about five seconds out of sync. Less than gymnastically my brother and I negotiated the wall and walked straight into the happy bedlam that was taking place. It was afterwards learned that Raith Rovers had struck the post in stoppage time. Quite literally the title had been won by the finest of margins.

Footballers are sometimes accused of lacking the same emotional commitment that the fans have but looking around Somerset Park at this time the players looked just as rabid as the most partisan of fans. Then the fans were requested to leave the field. This request was complied with meticulously in the knowledge that it was to allow the stage to be set up for the trophy presentation. Eyes were cast skyward to look for the helicopter. It then came over Somerset Park and landed at Ayr Racecourse from where the trophy was transported to the ground. The din reached a crescendo when it was presented to Steven Bell in his role as captain.

That night the official celebrations took place in Harleys in Nile Court, right next door to the building in which Ayr United were founded on 9th May, 1910. In the intervening 108 years a wealth of stories have been generated but what happened in 2017/18 could have been cast in fiction.

124 goals in competitive fixtures amounted to the second best of any season in the club's history. For season 2017/18 it also amounted to the best of any club in the British senior leagues. Manchester City came closest with 123 (domestic goals only – League 106, FA Cup 6 and Carabo Cup 11).

Literally and metaphorically it seemed a long way back from Alloa on that April Sunday. There are many who will testify that the league was won in the Ayr United way.

Games and Players 2017/18

Game 1. 5th August, 2017, Exsel Group Stadium:
Albion Rovers 1 Ayr United 5.
Team: Hart, Geggan, Reid, Higgins, Boyle, Crawford (McGuffie), McDaid, Adams (Rose), Docherty, Moffat (Forrest) and Moore; unused substitutes – Gilmour, Ferguson, Murphy and Avci.
Scorers: Declan McDaid, Michael Moffat and Craig Moore 3 (including a penalty).

Game 2. 12th August, 2017, Somerset Park:
Ayr United 3 Forfar Athletic 0.
Team: Hart, Geggan, Higgins, Rose, Boyle, McDaid (Gilmour), Docherty, Crawford, McGuffie (Reid), Moffat (Forrest) and Moore; unused substitutes –Ferguson, Faulds, Murphy and Avci.
Scorers: Craig Moore, Declan McDaid and Robbie Crawford.

Game 3. 19th August, 2017, Stair Park:
Stranraer 3 Ayr United 4.
Team: Hart, Geggan, Rose, Higgins, Boyle, McDaid (McGuffie), Crawford, Docherty, Reid, Moffat (Forrest) and Moore (Gilmour); unused substitutes –Ferguson and Avci.
Scorers: Declan McDaid, Craig Moore, Michael Moffat and Paddy Boyle.

Game 4. 26th August, 2017, Somerset Park:
Ayr United 1 Arbroath 2.
Team: Hart, Higgins, Boyle, Rose, Geggan, Moffat, Crawford (Gilmour), Moore, Forrest (Reid), McDaid and Docherty (McGuffie); unused substitutes –Ferguson, Murphy, McCowan and Avci.
Scorer: Chris Higgins.

Game 5. 9th September, 2017, Stark's Park:
Raith Rovers 2 Ayr United 1.
Team: Hart, Reid, Rose, Higgins, Ferguson, McDaid, Geggan, Crawford, McGuffie (Murphy), Moffat and Shankland (Gilmour); unused substitutes – Hilton, Faulds, Waite, McCowan and Avci.
Scorer: Lawrence Shankland.

Game 6. 16th September, 2017, Somerset Park:
Ayr United 3 Alloa Athletic 3.
Team: Hart, Geggan, Rose, Reid, Ferguson, McDaid, Docherty (Gilmour), Adams, McGuffie (Murphy), Moffat and Shankland; unused substitutes – Waite, McCowan and Avci.
Scorers: Lawrence Shankland 2 and Jamie Adams.

Game 7. 23rd September, 2017, Hampden Park:
Queen's Park 0 Ayr United 2.
Team: Hart, Geggan, Rose, Higgins, Reid, McDaid (McGuffie), Adams, Docherty, Gilmour (Murphy), Moffat (McCowan) and Shankland; unused substitutes –Ferguson and Avci.
Scorers: Jamie Adams and Lawrence Shankland.

Game 8. 30th September, 2017, Somerset Park:
Ayr United 3 East Fife 0.
Team: Hart, Higgins, Boyle, Gilmour, Rose, Geggan, Moffat, McDaid (McGuffie), Shankland, Docherty (Murphy) and Reid (Ferguson); unused substitutes – Balfour, McCowan and Avci.
Scorers: Lawrence Shankland, Andy Geggan and Chris Higgins.

Game 9. 14th October, 2017, Somerset Park:
Ayr United 2 Airdrie 2.
Team: Hart, Higgins, Boyle (Gilmour), Rose, Geggan, Moffat, Crawford, Ferguson, Shankland (Moore), Docherty and McGuffie (McDaid); unused substitutes – Forrest, McCowan and Avci.
Scorer: Andy Geggan 2.

Game 10. 21st October, 2017, Station Park:
Forfar Athletic 0 Ayr United 5.
Team: Hart, Ferguson, Higgins, Rose, Boyle, Crawford, Docherty, Geggan (McGuffie), Gilmour (McDaid), Moffat and Shankland (Moore); unused substitutes – Forrest, Waite, Murphy and Hare-Reid.
Scorers: Michael Moffat 3, Lawrence Shankland and Craig Moore.

Game 11. 28th October, 2017, Somerset Park:
Ayr United 2 Stranraer 0.
Team: Hart, Higgins, Boyle, Rose, Geggan (Adams), Moffat (Forrest), Crawford, McDaid (Moore), Ferguson, Shankland and Docherty; unused substitutes – Gilmour, McGuffie, Reid and Avci.
Scorers: Michael Moffat and Lawrence Shankland.

Game 12. 4th November, 2017, Gayfield Park:
Arbroath 1 Ayr United 4.
Team: Hart, Ferguson, Adams, Rose, Boyle, McDaid (Moore), Docherty, Geggan, Crawford, Moffat (Forrest) and Shankland (McGuffie); unused substitutes – Gilmour, Reid and Avci.
Scorers: Lawrence Shankland 2, David Gold – own goal and Craig Moore.

Game 13. 14th November, 2017, Somerset Park:
Ayr United 3 Raith Rovers 0.
Team: Hart, Higgins, Boyle, Rose, Geggan, Moffat (Moore), Crawford, Ferguson, Adams, Shankland (Forrest) and Docherty; unused substitutes – McDaid, McGuffie, Faulds, Reid and Avci.
Scorers: Lawrence Shankland, Robbie Crawford and Craig Moore.

Game 14. 25th November, 2017, Indodrill Stadium:
Alloa Athletic 1 Ayr United 2.
Team: Hart, Ferguson, Reid, Rose, Higgins, Geggan (McGuffie), Docherty, Crawford (Moore), Moffat (Forrest), Shankland and McDaid; unused substitutes – Gilmour, Faulds, Waite and Avci.
Scorers: Michael Moffat and Craig Moore.

Game 15. 2nd December, 2017, Somerset Park:
Ayr United 3 Albion Rovers 2.
Team: Hart, Reid, Ferguson, Rose, Higgins, Adams, Docherty (Forrest), Gilmour (McGuffie), Moffat, Moore (McDaid) and Shankland; unused substitutes –Faulds, Waite, Murphy and Avci.
Scorers: Craig Moore, Lawrence Shankland and Chris Higgins.

Game 16. 9th December, 2017, Somerset Park:
Ayr United 3 Queen's Park 2.
Team: Hart, Higgins, Gilmour, Rose, Moffat, Moore (McDaid), McGuffie (Forrest), Ferguson, Adams, Shankland and Reid (Boyle); unused substitutes – Hilton, Faulds, Docherty and Avci.
Scorers: Craig Moore (penalty), Declan McDaid and Alan Forrest.

Game 17. 16th December, 2017, Bayview Stadium:
East Fife 1 Ayr United 4.
Team: Hart, Ferguson, Higgins, Rose, Boyle, Forrest (McGuffie), Geggan, Adams (Gilmour), McDaid (Moore), Moffat and Shankland; unused substitutes – Faulds, Murphy, Reid, Avci.
Scorers: Michael Rose 2, Craig Moore and Lawrence Shankland.

Game 18. 23rd December, 2017, Shyberry Excelsior Stadium:
Airdrie 2 Ayr United 0.
Team: Hart, Ferguson, Rose, Higgins, Boyle (Murphy), Forrest (McGuffie), Geggan (McDaid), Gilmour, Moore, Shankland and Moffat; unused substitutes – Hilton, Faulds, Reid and Avci.

Game 19. 30th December, 2017, Somerset Park:
Ayr United 2 Forfar Athletic 3.
Team: Hart, Higgins, Boyle, Gilmour, Rose, Geggan (Adams), Moffat, Forrest, McDaid (McGuffie), Ferguson and Shankland (Moore); unused substitutes – Faulds, Murphy, Reid and Avci.
Scorers: Michael Moffat and Lawrence Shankland.

Game 20. 2nd January, 2018, Stair Park:
Stranraer 1 Ayr United 5.
Team: Hart, Ferguson, Higgins, Rose (Faulds), Boyle, McDaid, Reid, Adams, Forrest (Hilton), Shankland and Moffat (Moore); unused substitutes – Gilmour, McGuffie, McCowan and Avci.
Scorers: Lawrence Shankland 2, Michael Moffat, Alan Forrest 2.

Game 21. 6th January, 2018, Somerset Park:
Ayr United 1 Arbroath 2.
Team: Hart, Higgins (Faulds), Boyle, Moffat, Forrest; McDaid (Moore), Ferguson, Adams, Shankland, Reid and Bell; unused substitutes – Hilton, Balfour, Murphy, McCowan and Avci.
Scorer: Alan Forrest.

Game 22. 13th January, 2018, Stark's Park:
Raith Rovers 1 Ayr United 1.
Team: Ruddy, Ferguson, Reid, Rose, Boyle, McDaid, Adams (Moore), Bell, Forrest, Moffat and Shankland; unused substitutes – McGuffie, Hilton, Faulds, Murphy, McCowan and Hart.
Scorer: Lawrence Shankland.

Game 23. 27th January, 2018, Hampden Park:
Queen's Park 1 Ayr United 4.
Team: Ruddy, Boyle, Rose, Moore (Moffat), Forrest (McGuffie), McDaid, Ferguson, Adams (Geggan), Shankland, Reid and Kerr; unused substitutes – Faulds, Murphy, McCowan and Hart.
Scorers: Craig Moore, Alan Forrest and Craig McGuffie 2.

Game 24. 3rd February, 2018, Somerset Park:
Ayr United 1 Alloa Athletic 2.
Team: Ruddy, Boyle, Rose, Moffat, Forrest (McGuffie), McDaid, Ferguson (Moore), Shankland, Reid, Kerr (Adams) and Bell; unused substitutes – Faulds, Murphy, McCowan and Hart.
Scorer: Lawrence Shankland.

Game 25. 17th February, 2018, Somerset Park:
Ayr United 3 East Fife 0.
Team: Ruddy, Boyle, Rose, Moffat, Forrest (McGuffie), McDaid, Ferguson (Moore), Shankland, Reid, Kerr (Adams) and Bell; unused substitutes – Faulds, Murphy, McCowan and Hart.
Scorers: Declan McDaid, Lawrence Shankland and Alan Forrest (penalty).

Game 26. 24th February, 2018, Somerset Park:
Ayr United 3 Airdrie 0.
Team: Ruddy, Geggan, Bell, Rose, Boyle, McDaid, Kerr (Docherty), Adams, Forrest (Crawford), Moore (Moffat) and Shankland; unused substitutes – Reid, Ferguson, McGuffie and Hart.
Scorers: Andy Geggan and Lawrence Shankland 2 (including a penalty).

Game 27. 10th March, 2018, Somerset Park:
Ayr United 3 Raith Rovers 0.
Team: Ruddy, Boyle (Ferguson), Rose, Geggan, Moffat, Crawford (Reid), McDaid, Adams, Shankland, Kerr (Docherty) and Bell; unused substitutes – Moore, Forrest, McGuffie and Hart.
Scorers: Lawrence Shankland, Jamie Adams and Michael Moffat.

Game 28. 14th March, 2018, Gayfield Park:
Arbroath 1 Ayr United 1.
Team: Ruddy, Geggan, Bell, Rose, Reid, McDaid (Forrest), Kerr, Adams, Crawford (McGuffie), Moffat (Moore) and Shankland; unused substitutes – Ferguson, Docherty and Hart.
Scorer: Craig McGuffie.

Game 29. 17th March, 2018, Station Park:
Forfar Athletic 0 Ayr United 2.
Team: Ruddy, Boyle, Rose, Geggan, Moffat (Moore), Crawford, Forrest, McDaid (McGuffie), Shankland, Kerr and Bell; unused substitutes – Ferguson, Docherty, Reid and Hart.
Scorers: Michael Moffat and Craig Moore (penalty).

Game 30. 17th March, 2018, Cliftonhill Stadium:
Albion Rovers 2 Ayr United 3.
Team: Ruddy, Boyle, Rose, Geggan, Crawford, Moore (Moffat), Forrest (McGuffie), Adams, Shankland, Kerr and Bell; unused substitutes – McDaid, Ferguson, Docherty, Reid and Hart.
Scorers: Craig Moore, Jamie Adams and Lawrence Shankland.

Game 31. 24th March, 2018, Somerset Park:
Ayr United 4 Queen's Park 0.
Team: Ruddy, Boyle, Rose, Reid, Moffat, Crawford, Forrest (McGuffie), McDaid, Shankland (Faulds), Kerr (Moore) and Bell; unused substitutes – Ferguson, Murphy and Hart.
Scorers: Lawrence Shankland 3 and Craig Moore (penalty).

After his magnificent season Lawrence Shankland signed a new contract — to the delight of Ian McCall and every Ayr United supporter

Game 32. 31st March, 2018, Bayview Stadium:
East Fife 2 Ayr United 3.
Team: Ruddy, Reid, Rose, Bell, Boyle, Forrest, Crawford (Moffat), Kerr and McDaid (McGuffie), Moore (Adams) and Shankland; unused substitutes – Ferguson, Faulds, McCowan and Hart.
Scorers: Alan Forrest, Steven Bell and Craig Moore (penalty).

Game 33. 7th April, 2018, Shyberry Excelsior Stadium:
Airdrie 1 Ayr United 2.
Team: Hart, Geggan (Ferguson), Reid, Bell, Boyle (Forrest), McDaid (McGuffie), Adams, Kerr, Crawford, Moore and Shankland; unused substitutes –Faulds, Murphy, McCowan and Ruddy.
Scorers: Robbie Crawford and Lawrence Shankland.

Game 34. 14th April, 2018, Somerset Park:
Ayr United 1 Stranraer 2.
Team: Hart, Ferguson, Bell, Rose, Reid (McGuffie then Moffat for McGuffie), Crawford, Adams, Kerr, Forrest (McDaid), Shankland and Moore; unused substitutes –Faulds, Murphy, McCowan and Hare-Reid.
Scorer: Jamie Adams.

Game 35. 22nd April, 2018, Indodrill Stadium:
Alloa Athletic 2 Ayr United 1.
Team: Hart, Geggan (McGuffie), Bell, Rose, Ferguson, McDaid (Forrest), Kerr, Adams, Crawford, Moffat and Moore; unused substitutes –Faulds, Murphy, McCowan and Hare-Reid.
Scorer: Craig Moore.

Game 36. 28th April, 2018, Somerset Park:
Ayr United 2 Albion Rovers 0.
Team: Hart, Rose, Adams, Bell, Ferguson, McDaid, Kerr, Crawford, Forrest (McGuffie), Moffat and Moore; unused substitutes –Faulds, Murphy, McCowan and Hare-Reid.
Scorers: Craig Moore and Declan McDaid.

League One top three 2017/18

	P	W	D	L	F	A	Points
Ayr United	36	24	4	8	92	42	76
Raith Rovers	36	22	9	5	68	32	75
Alloa Athletic	36	17	9	10	56	43	60

League goals

Lawrence Shankland	26	Chris Higgins	3
Craig Moore	19	Craig McGuffie	3
Michael Moffat	11	Michael Rose	2
Alan Forrest	7	Steven Bell	1
Declan McDaid	6	Paddy Boyle	1
Jamie Adams	5	David Gold	
Andy Geggan	4	(Arbroath)	1 own goal
Robbie Crawford	3	**Total**	**92**

2017/18 – The Main Stats

League One champions.
124 goals – 2nd highest in the club's history.
The first club in the British leagues to hit a century.
The highest total of domestic goals of any club in the British leagues.
Club record away win in the League Cup.
Club record fastest goal.
Fifteen League Cup goals in a season = a club best since 1980/81.
Opening league game hat-trick for the first time since 1970.
Equalled the club record winning margin in the Irn Bru Cup/Challenge Cup.
Second biggest opening away league win in our history.
The first player to score in his first four competitive matches for the club.
Club record fastest goal in a Scottish Cup tie.
Nine consecutive wins = the third best in the club's history.
One point short of the club record points total.
League One Player of the Year = Lawrence Shankland.
League One Manager of the Year = Ian McCall.
First title win at home since 1928.
No visiting team left Somerset Park with a clean sheet.
Scored in all except two games = a club record shared with 1936/37.
Five goals or more in three consecutive matches for the first time since 1953.
The largest number of Ayr United captains in a season with four.
The first club to get a sponsorship deal in cryptocurrency.
32 goals in the first nine games = a club best since 1911/12.
League One Manager and Player of the Month = three wins in each category.

Our League Titles – When and Where

1912 — Clinched with a 4-0 home win over Albion Rovers.
1913 — Title retained after the club had completed its fixtures. Abercorn still had five matches left and needed seven points. When they lost 5-1 away to East Stirling it was Ayr United's title.
1928 — Clinched on the day we lost 1-0 at home to Dumbarton.
1937 — Clinched on the day we drew 2-2 away to Raith Rovers.
1959 — Clinched on the night Arbroath lost to Stenhousemuir and we had no game.
1966 — Clinched with a 4-0 win at Stenhousemuir.
1988 — Clinched with a 3-1 win away to Alloa Athletic.
1997 — Clinched with a 2-0 win away to Berwick Rangers.
2018 — Clinched with a 2-0 win at home to Albion Rovers.

A century in competitive matches

Ayr United have exceeded a century of goals in a season seven times. Commiserations to the team of 1968/69 for finishing on ninety-nine. Please note that only competitive matches have been taken into account. Friendlies, Charity Cup matches and Ayrshire Cup ties are typical of the exclusions.

Season	Goals	Games
1958/59:	139	46 games
2017/18:	124	46 games
1936/37:	122	35 games
1927/28:	121	40 games
1955/56:	118	44 games
1957/58:	114	44 games
1987/88:	104	44 games

The highest ratio was in 1936/37. 1927/28 and 1958/59 are the only other seasons in which a ratio exceeding three has been reached.

A century of goals in a season: the landmark scorers

Below is a list of players who have hit goal number 100 and when they did it. Peter Price is the only double entry on the list in addition to which he hit goal ninety-nine in 1958/59. In order that a comparison can be made it was thought useful to document the number of games taken to reach the landmark. On six of the seven occasions the century has been struck at Somerset Park.

Jimmy Smith: 25th February, 1928: Our second goal in a 7-3 league win at home to Arbroath. Game 32.

Hyam Dimmer: 13th February, 1937: Our first goal in a 5-2 league win at home to St.Bernard's. Game 29.

Peter Price: 24th March, 1956: The only goal in a 1-0 league win at home to Dundee United. Game 37.

Peter Price: 8th March, 1958: Our second goal in a 3-3 league draw at home to Arbroath. Game 37.

Alastair McIntyre: 24th January, 1959: Our third goal in a 4-0 league win against Queen's Park at Hampden. Game 31.

John Sludden: 9th April, 1988: Our third goal in a 3-1 league win at home to Stranraer. Game 41.

Andy Geggan: 24th February, 2018: Our first goal in a 3-0 league win at home to Airdrie. Game 36.

Index

A

Abercorn 7, 8, 9, 15, 17, 19, 23, 27, 29, 30, 232
Aberdeen 107, 204
Adams, Jamie 115, 201, 202, 207, 211, 213, 215, 219, 221, 222, 223, 224, 225, 226, 228, 229
Agnew, Scott 215
Airdrie 27, 54, 57, 60, 88, 91, 93, 99, 102, 104, 107, 153, 195, 197, 202, 203, 205, 210, 213, 214, 222, 224, 225, 228, 233
Aitken, Sam 23, 25, 27, 29, 30, 31, 32, 33
Albion Rovers xiii, 11, 15, 19, 23, 27, 29, 33, 37, 44, 47, 75, 80, 91, 97, 101, 113, 115, 116, 117, 126, 130, 135, 136, 139, 151, 197, 200, 202, 204, 210, 211, 213, 214, 217, 218, 219, 221, 223, 226, 228, 232
Allan (1936/37) 60
Allan, Willie 29, 30, 31, 33
Alloa Athletic v, xiii, 44, 47, 57, 60, 65, 66, 67, 75, 80, 93, 99, 102, 107, 115, 120, 128, 134, 135, 196, 201, 204, 206, 208, 215, 216, 217, 218, 220, 222, 223, 225, 228, 229, 232
Anderson, Euan 202
Anderson, Grant 215
Annan Athletic 107, 192, 195
Annbank 11
Arbroath 41, 45, 48, 69, 77, 80, 82, 91, 93, 101, 104, 109, 117, 119, 128, 132, 135, 199, 202, 203, 206, 207, 208, 211, 212, 213, 214, 219, 221, 223, 224, 226, 229, 232, 233
Ardeer Works 34
Ardrossan Winton Rovers 65
Armadale 46, 49
Arsenal 65, 107, 108
Arthurlie 9, 17, 25, 27, 29, 31, 37, 39, 44, 47
Aston Villa 123
Avci, Lyle 193, 221, 222, 223, 224
Ayr Advertiser v, 37, 42, 53, 54, 88, 93, 109, 115
Ayr Albion 65
Ayr and District League 5
Ayr Charity Cup 4, 11, 232
Ayr FC 3, 23, 123, 218
Ayr Guildry Cup 199
Ayrshire and Galloway Hotel 28
Ayrshire Cup 11, 88, 93, 123, 173, 232
Ayrshire Post v, 3, 9, 11, 13, 27, 39, 42, 65, 67, 69, 91
Ayr Town Hall 37
Ayr United Brake Club 7
Ayr United Juniors 5, 23
Ayr United Supporters' Association 202
Ayr United Supporters' Club 37

B

Baillieston Juniors 65
Balfour, John 101, 102, 104
Balfour, Kieran 193, 222, 224

Ballantyne, Jamie 193
Banks O' Dee 203
Barrhead 9, 37
Bathgate 44, 48
Bayern Munich 173
Bayview Park, Methil 48, 61, 77, 102
Bayview Stadium, Methil 214, 224, 228
BBC Alba 213, 216
Bell, Bobby 170
Bell, Robert 162, 170, 186, 187,
Bell, Steven 203, 206, 207, 210, 212, 214, 220, 224, 225, 226, 228, 229
Benburb 157
Benedictus, Kyle 211
Beresford Park, Ayr 3, 5, 11, 23
Berwick Rangers 67, 73, 79, 91, 99, 102, 111, 117, 124, 128, 132, 138, 139, 144, 157, 159, 162, 163, 165, 166, 167, 170, 173, 174, 181, 186, 187, 206, 232
Biggart, Kevin 147, 174, 176, 177, 188
Birmingham City 147
Black, Willie 11, 15, 16, 17, 19, 29, 30, 31
Black (1936/37) 57
Blackburn Rovers 139
Boca Juniors 3
Boghead Park, Dumbarton 17, 27, 32, 46, 58, 75, 103, 177, 181, 218
Bo'ness 41
Bourhill, Robert 56, 57
Bowey, Steve 115
Boyd, Andy 69
Boyle, Paddy 199, 201, 203, 207, 210, 214, 221, 222, 223, 224, 225, 226, 228, 229
B & Q Cup 165
Bradford City 53
Brae, Billy 39, 44, 45, 46, 47, 48, 49, 50
Brand, Ralph 144
Brechin City 54, 58, 60, 67, 75, 79, 88, 93, 97, 103, 109, 113, 114, 123,

126, 130, 136, 143, 144, 153, 167, 169, 170, 174, 179, 184, 187
Broadwood Stadium, Cumbernaild 165, 167, 179, 187
Brogan, John 119
Broomfield Park, Airdrie 57, 88, 99, 113, 130
Broomloan Road 142
Brown (St.Johnstone) 9
Brown, Bobby 69
Brown, Robert 120, 135, 136
BT Sports 193
Buchanan, Archie 35, 53
Buckie Thistle 197
Burgess, Michael 170
Burn, Ramsay 81
Burns Cottage v, 194
Burns, Robert 159
Burns, Gordon 177

C

Cairns, Dean 211
Callaghan Tom 155
"Cameron" (1927/28) 50
Cameron, Justin 142
Campbell, Archie 15, 16, 17, 19, 29, 30, 31, 32, 33
Campbell, Dick 199, 208
Campbell, Iain 199
Campsie Black Watch 139
Camsell, George 42
Cappielow Park, Greenock 39, 45, 57, 80, 111
Carrick, Dale 214
Carson, Joe 115
Carson Thistle 5
Castilla, David 157, 175, 181, 184
Cathkin Park, Glasgow 42, 49, 99
Cattle Market Inn 42
Caven, Ross 117
Cawley, Kevin 201, 216
Celtic xiii, 13, 25, 41
Central Park, Cowdenbeath 56, 79, 97, 109, 126

Challenge Cup 144, 153, 231
Chapman, Jim 113
Chelsea 7
Cherry, Paul 115
Christie, Norman 170
City Park, Edinburgh 58
Clancy, Dan 56, 57
Clark, Gary 151
Clark, John 155, 181
Clarke, John 155
Cliftonhill Park, Coatbridge 47, 75, 101, 113, 151, 165, 177, 197, 226
Cliftonville 53
Clyde 54, 147, 153, 157, 161, 162, 165, 167, 174, 179, 184, 187, 195
Clydebank 37, 45, 48, 107, 139
Clydeholm Park 45
Coatbridge 19, 197, 213
Coburn, Jacky 88, 97, 99, 101, 104
Connell, Willie 15, 16, 17, 19, 29, 30, 31, 32
Connor, Robert 142, 151, 155, 174, 177, 179, 181, 188
Cook, Barry 207
Cowdenbeath, 15, 19, 23, 27, 29, 30, 56, 60, 65, 67, 68, 73, 79, 82, 88, 91, 97, 101, 109, 112, 113, 115, 117, 126, 130, 134
Cowell, Jim 120, 124, 126, 128, 130, 132, 134, 135, 136
Cox, Jacky 63, 65, 69, 71
Coyle, Kevin 173
Coyle, Ronnie 139, 151, 153, 167, 170, 173, 174, 176, 177, 179, 181, 183, 184, 186, 187
Coyle, Tommy 111
Craigmark Smithfield 5
Crane, Callum 216
Crawford, Robbie 201, 203, 206, 210, 214, 221, 222, 223, 225, 226, 228, 229
Crawford, Stevie 142
Cummings, John 102, 104
Cummins, Adam 208
Currie, Davy 56, 57, 58, 59, 60, 61, 62

D

Daily Record 27, 119
Dalziel, Gordon 137, 139, 142, 144, 147, 153, 157, 162, 165, 167, 174, 180, 181
Darvel 91
"Davidson" (1911/12) 19
Davidson, Iain 207
Dean, Dixie 42
Dean, James 44, 49
Denholm, Danny 212
Devlin, Nicky 191
Dickson (1911/12) 15, 17
Dimmer, Hyam 55, 56, 57, 58, 59, 60, 61, 233
Docherty, Ross 195, 201, 203, 206, 210, 221, 222, 223, 224, 225, 226
Donald, Michael 212
Donnelly, Luke 202
Douglas Park, Hamilton 77
Douglas, Rab 155, 162
Duggan, Chris 205, 214
Dumbarton 3, 5, 9, 10, 11, 16, 17, 19, 25, 26, 27, 28, 31, 32, 37, 39, 41, 42, 46, 49, 58, 59, 67, 69, 75, 81, 93, 99, 103, 104, 109, 147, 151, 153, 157, 159, 160, 162, 165, 177, 181, 186, 188, 195, 203, 218, 232
Dumbarton Harp 37
Dumfries 5
Dundee 65, 199
Dundee Hibernian 3, 5, 7, 11, 15, 16, 25, 29, 31
Dundee United 3, 41, 42, 46, 49, 57, 59, 75, 80, 147, 208, 233
Dunfermline Athletic 25, 27, 30, 32, 33, 69, 115, 120, 155, 191, 197, 199
Dunterlie Park, Barrhead 17, 29, 44
Duthie, Mark 162, 164
Dyer, Jimmy 56, 58, 60

E

East End Park, Dunfermline 30
Easter Road, Edinburgh 197
East Fife 42, 45, 48, 54, 55, 57, 61, 69, 70, 77, 81, 93, 95, 102, 104, 153, 157, 202, 203, 204, 205, 210, 213, 214, 222, 224, 225, 228
East Kilbride Juveniles 120
East Stirling 15, 19, 25, 27, 30, 31, 33, 37, 42, 46, 49, 54, 56, 59, 69, 77, 81, 93, 101, 103, 115, 118, 123, 128, 132, 136, 155, 195, 197, 199, 218, 232
Edgar, Derek 115
Edinburgh 53, 117, 139
Edinburgh City 53, 56, 58
Elder, Graeme 115
English, Isaac 142, 151, 155, 157, 174, 176, 177, 179, 181, 182, 188
English League 3, 5
Evans, Stevie 124, 126, 128, 130, 132, 134, 135, 136
Exsel Group Stadium, Coatbridge 221

F

FA Cup 7, 53, 220
Fairlie (1911/12) 17, 19
Falkirk 41, 69, 107, 155, 208
Faulds, Stuart 193, 221, 223, 224, 225, 226, 228
Ferguson, David 193, 217, 221, 222, 223, 224, 225, 226, 228
Feroz, Craig 167
Finnie, Stephen 213
Fir Park, Motherwell 165, 187
Firs Park, Falkirk 46, 56, 69, 81, 103, 128
Fisher, Bud 53, 56, 61
Flannigan, Iain 216
Fleming, Willie 41, 42, 44, 45, 46, 47, 48, 49, 50
Foderingham, Wes 210
Fog 77, 159
Forbes, Neil 115
Forfar Athletic 45, 48, 56, 59, 65, 67, 69, 77, 81, 88, 97, 103, 123, 159, 197, 202, 203, 205, 206, 207, 211, 212, 221, 222, 224, 226
Forrest, Alan 196, 201, 204, 206, 208, 210, 213, 221, 222, 223, 224, 225, 226, 228, 229
Forthbank, Stirling 44, 58
Fulton, Billy 73, 75, 77, 82
Fulton, Jim 65, 73
Furphy, Willie 107, 120, 124, 126, 128, 130, 132, 134, 135, 136

G

Gaiety Theatre 42
Galabank, Annan 107, 192
Galston 23, 91
Galt, David 202
Garden, Stuart 167
Gardiner (1911/12) 5, 15
Gayfield Park, Arbroath 45, 80, 104, 132, 212, 223, 226
Geggan, Andy 191, 195, 201, 206, 210, 211, 213, 221, 222, 223, 224, 225, 226, 228, 229, 233
Geller, Uri 157
Gemmell, David 56, 57, 58, 59, 60, 61
Gemson, Lawrence 42
George, Duncan 144, 147, 156, 157, 174, 177, 181, 184, 187, 188
Gibson, Tommy 81
Gibson, William 57, 61
Gillespie, Alex 37
Gilmour, Brian 206, 221, 222, 223, 224
Girvan Athletic 23
Glasgow Herald 109
Glasgow Rangers xiii, 5, 37, 119, 144, 210
Glebe Park, Brechin 60, 75, 103, 126, 136, 144, 157, 174, 184

Glen, Alex 65, 73, 75, 77, 79, 80, 81, 82
Gold (1911/12) 17
Gold, David 223, 229
Goodwin, Hilly 11, 14, 15, 16, 17, 19, 30, 31, 32, 33
Graham, Andy 201
Grant, Johnny 85, 97, 99, 101, 102, 103, 104
Guinness Book of Records 37
Gymnasium Ground, The, Edinburgh 19, 32, 47, 58

H

Hamilton Accies 11, 65, 67, 69, 77, 80, 140, 141, 144, 145, 151, 155, 157, 159, 162, 165, 167, 170, 174, 177, 178, 181, 187, 188
Hamilton, Ian 65, 73, 75, 77, 79, 80, 81, 82
Hampden Park, Glasgow 79, 99, 130, 202, 208, 218, 219, 222, 225, 233
Hare-Reid, Ellis 222, 228
Hart, Jordan 202, 205, 206, 214, 216, 221, 222, 223, 224, 225, 226, 228
Haugh, Adam 80, 81
Hawkshaw, Ian 85, 93, 97, 99, 101, 102, 103, 104
Hearts 67, 142, 199, 215
Heddle, Ian 111
Henderson, Darren 142, 150, 162, 174, 176, 177, 179, 181, 184, 186, 187, 188
Hendry, Willie 73, 81
Hepburn, Bob 39, 41, 44, 45, 46, 47, 48, 49, 50
Hernon, Daniel 56
Hester, Kane 213
Hewitt, Scott 139
Hibernian 85, 195, 199, 205, 215
Higgins, Chris 191, 201, 203, 204, 206, 210, 221, 222, 223, 224, 229
Higgins, Sean 213, 219
High Street 7

Hilton, James 193, 221, 224, 225
Hodge, William 19
Holt, John 115
Hood, Gregg 142, 151, 157, 162, 174, 177, 181, 184, 186, 187, 188
Horace, Alain 141, 153, 155, 159, 160, 165, 167, 170, 179, 181, 184, 186, 187, 188
Howe, Charlie 201
Huddersfield Town 147
Hughes, Jim 120, 124, 126, 128, 130, 132, 134, 135, 136
Humphries, Mark 153, 170, 178, 179, 181, 184, 186, 187
Hurlford 11, 23

I

Ibrox Stadium, Glasgow 142
Indodrill Stadium, Alloa 223, 228
Inglis (1927/28) 48
Irvine Valley 91
Irish Cup 53
Irn Bru Cup 197, 199, 203, 231

J

Jack, Ross 115
"Jackson" (1927/28) 48
Jamieson, Willie 139, 147, 163, 167, 174, 176, 179, 181, 184, 186, 187, 188
Jefferies, Jim 142
Johnstone FC 27, 30, 32

K

Kenmuir, Michael 57
Kennedy, David 128
Kerr, Billy 97, 99
Kerr, Mark 194, 208, 210, 211, 225, 226, 228
Kerrigan, Stevie 139, 142, 147, 151, 153, 157, 162, 166, 168, 174, 177, 179, 181, 184, 186, 187, 188

Kilmarnock 88, 123, 142, 173, 193, 195, 199
Kilpatrick, Tommy 40, 44, 45, 46, 47, 48, 49, 50
King's Park 44, 48, 50, 55, 58, 61
Kinnaird, Paul 142, 147, 153, 171, 174, 177, 179, 181, 184, 186, 187, 188
Kirkcaldy xiii, 202, 207, 210, 216, 218
Kirkintilloch Rob Roy 65
Kirkmichael Amateurs 85
Klinsmann, Jurgen 173

L

Law, Bobby 151, 174, 177, 179, 181, 184
League Cup 65, 67, 88, 142, 144, 193, 195, 197, 199, 205, 231
League One 189, 190, 191, 199, 203, 204, 208, 229, 231
League Two 191
Leith Athletic 7, 16, 30, 31, 42, 47, 50, 53, 54, 56, 59, 61
Lennox, Aaron 211
Levein, Craig 215
Lindsay Hicks 69
Links Park, Montrose 56, 73, 97, 128, 134
Linthouse 23
Livingston 142, 147, 151, 153, 155, 157, 159, 162, 164, 165, 167, 170, 173, 177, 180, 181, 184, 186, 188
Logan, Hugh 15, 16, 17, 19
Logie Green, Edinburgh 16, 31
Lowland League 197
Lowrie, Ronnie 120
Luton Town 142

Mac/Mc

MacDonald, Allan 117
MacLeod 54, 85, 105, 107, 111, 113, 115, 120, 121
McAllister, Ian 107, 111, 120, 122, 123, 124, 126, 128, 129, 130, 132, 134, 135, 136
McAnespie, Alex 85, 93, 97, 99, 100, 101, 102, 103, 104
McCall, Andy 47, 49
McCall, Ian 189, 191, 202, 205, 208, 210, 215, 227, 231
McCann, Jim 115, 117, 120, 124, 128, 130, 132, 134, 135, 136
McCart, Jamie 208
McColgan, Felix 39, 44, 45, 46, 47, 48, 49, 50
McCormick, Steve 167
McCosh, John 44, 47
McCowan, Luke 193, 221, 222, 224, 225, 228
McCracken, Dougie 115, 124, 126, 128, 130, 132, 134, 136
McCreath, Tom 83, 85
McCrossan, Gerry 20, 29, 30
McCulloch, Scott 167
McCulloch, Willie 142, 186
McDaid, Declan 195, 197, 204, 210, 211, 219, 221, 222, 223, 224, 225, 226, 228, 229
McGhee, Jim 65, 73, 75, 77, 78, 79, 80, 81, 82
McGibbons, Terry 54, 56, 57, 58, 59, 60, 61
McGowan (St.Johnstone) 9
McGowan, Henry 29, 30, 31, 32, 33
McGuffie, Craig 196, 206, 208, 212, 214, 217, 221, 222, 223, 224, 225, 226, 228, 229
McIntosh, Leighton 206
McIntosh, Martin 151, 167
McIntyre, Alastair 67, 73, 75, 77, 79, 80, 81, 82, 233
McIntyre, George 72, 79, 81, 82
McIntyre, Stevie 120, 124, 126, 128, 130, 132, 134, 135, 136, 233
McIntyre, Willie 73, 75, 77, 79, 80, 81, 82

McKenna (1912/13) 30, 31
McKenzie, Hugh 5, 15, 17
McKenzie, Alan, 113
McKenzie, Paul 113, 117, 124, 128, 130, 132, 134, 135, 136
McKenzie, Robert 113
McLafferty, Martin 120
McLaughlan, Switcher 5, 9, 11, 15, 16, 17, 19, 25, 29, 30, 31, 32, 33
McLean, Jim 65, 73, 75, 76, 77, 79, 80, 81, 82
McLean, Tommy 147
McMillan, Sam 73, 75, 77, 79, 80, 81, 82, 87, 93, 96, 97, 99, 101, 102, 103, 104
McNeill, John 56
McNiven, John 119
McQueen, Eric 119
McStay, Jock 25, 153, 179, 181, 186, 187
McStay, Willie 25, 30, 31, 32, 153
McVey, Conor 204

M

Magee, Lewis 204
Malcolm, Craig 201
Malone, Dick 85, 97, 98, 99, 101, 102, 103, 104
Manchester City 147, 203, 220
Manchester United 41, 65
Marshall, Davy 91
Massey, Lee 5, 15, 16, 17, 19, 23, 29, 31
Mathie, Graeme 215
Maybole 85
Maybole Juniors 65, 113
Mayes, Jock 54, 58, 59, 60, 61
Meadowbank, Edinburgh 54, 59
Meadowbank Thistle 107, 218
Meadow Park, Coatbridge 11, 29
Meechan, Jim 153
Meggatt, Daryll 201
Melville, Jimmy 44

Mercer, Jim 139, 147, 174, 177, 179, 181, 188
Merchiston Park, Falkirk 19, 30
Methil 214
Middlesbrough 23, 25, 42
Millar, Ian 97, 99, 101, 102, 103, 104
Millburn Park, Alexandria 15, 32
Millen, Ross 202
Mill Park, Bathgate 44
Millwall 142
Moffat, Michael 191, 202, 207, 211, 213, 219, 221, 222, 223, 224, 225, 226, 228, 229
Monan, Eddie 85, 95, 97, 99, 101, 102, 103, 104
Montrose 53, 54, 56, 67, 73, 88, 91, 97, 101, 109, 111, 115, 124, 128, 134, 199
Mooney, Patrick 17, 19, 30, 31, 32
Moore, Craig 191, 196, 197, 201, 203, 204, 205, 207, 208, 213, 214, 217, 219, 221, 222, 223, 224, 225, 226, 228, 229
Moore, Eddie 93, 97, 99, 102, 103, 104,
Morrison (Stenhousemuir) 39
Morton 39, 45, 47, 55, 57, 61, 69, 73, 80, 193, 195, 201, 206
Mossblown Strollers 23
Motherwell 165, 193
Muirton Park, Perth 9, 81, 117, 124, 134
Mulhouse 153
Mullin, Michael 219
Murphy, John 91, 97, 99, 101, 102, 103, 104
Murphy, Leon 193, 221, 222, 223, 224, 225, 226, 228
Murphy, Peter 195
Murray, Euan 207
Murray, Harry 1, 21, 53
Murray, Gary 115

N

Neill, Morgyn 215
Newall, Jock 60
Newall, Tom 30, 31, 32, 33
Newcastle 42
Newfield, Johnstone 27, 32
Newmilns 91
Newton 3
Nice 157
Nisbet, Jim 41, 44, 45, 46, 47, 48, 49, 50
North End Park, Cowdenbeath 15, 29
Norway 43

O

O'Brien, Thomas 206
Ochilview Park, Larbert 39, 46, 57, 73, 104, 109, 126, 136, 154, 174, 184, 199
Oldham Athletic 147
Oliphant, Charlie 85, 97, 99, 101, 102, 103, 104
Oslo 43

P

Page (1912/13) 29, 31
Page, Jonathan 205
Palais de Danse 37
Palmerston Park, Dumfries 48, 101, 147, 177, 184
Parkhouse 3
Parry, Neil 217
Partick Thistle 67, 151, 193, 195
Paterson, Alex 73, 75, 77, 79, 82
Paterson, Arthur 85, 91, 97, 99, 101, 102, 103, 104
Paterson, Davy 88, 97, 102, 104
Paton, Alastair 97, 99, 101
Paton, Willie 73, 75, 77, 79, 80, 81, 82
Peacock, James 29, 30, 32, 33
Peddie, Alec 16
Phillips, Charlie 5, 7, 15, 16, 17, 19, 25, 29, 30, 31, 32, 33

Popplewell, Ben 42
Port Glasgow Athletic 5
Powderhall, Edinburgh 50
Preston North End 9
Price, Norman 49,
Price, Peter 65, 67, 73, 75, 77, 79, 80, 81, 82, 111, 159, 233
Provost Gould 37
Pullar, John 104
Purdie, David 107
Purdon (1927/28) 44, 45, 46, 47, 48, 49, 50

Q

Queen of the South 45, 48, 88, 91, 92, 93, 97, 101, 107, 147, 152, 153, 155, 158, 159, 168, 172, 177, 179, 184, 186, 191, 199
Queen's Park 67, 75, 79, 82, 99, 102, 115, 117, 119, 126, 130, 134, 136, 167, 197, 202, 204, 205, 208, 209, 213, 215, 218, 219, 222, 224, 225, 226, 233

R

Raith Rovers xiii, 23, 55, 60, 61, 99, 103, 142, 144, 147, 153, 155, 173, 191, 199, 201, 202, 203, 206, 207, 208, 210, 211, 212, 213, 214, 215, 216, 217, 218, 219, 220, 221, 223, 225, 226, 229, 232
Ralston Park, Paisley 17, 30
Reading 107, 110
Recreation Ground, Perth 9, 17, 31
Recreation Park 47, 60, 80, 102, 134, 135
Reid, Craig 204, 207, 221, 222, 223, 224, 225, 226, 228
Richardson (Leith Athletic) 53, 56, 61
Ritchie, Paul 165
River Plate 3
Robertson, Jacky 197

Robertson, Jimmy 7, 9, 16, 17, 19
Robertson, Willie 41, 44, 45, 46, 47, 48, 49, 50
Rodgers, Alan 135, 136
Rose, Michael 202, 205, 206, 221, 222, 223, 224, 225, 226, 228, 229
Ross County 155, 199
Ruddy, Jack 207, 210, 214, 225, 226, 228
Rugby Park, Kilmarnock 23, 142, 193
Rutherford, Paul 120

S

St.Bernard's 9, 17, 19, 27, 30, 32, 37, 44, 47, 54, 55, 58, 60, 61, 233
St.Johnstone 5, 9, 12, 17, 31, 32, 69, 77, 81, 85, 91, 109, 111, 113, 117, 119, 123, 124, 128, 134, 136, 144, 197
St.Mirren 13, 27, 107, 155, 201
St.Mirren Park, Paisley 23
Scally, Neil 210
Scott, Archie 202
Scott, Dougie 144
Scott, Robert 157, 165, 167, 170, 178, 181, 184, 186, 187, 188
Scott, Ross 113, 124, 126, 128, 130, 132, 134, 135, 136
Scottish Alliance 37
Scottish Cup 25, 27, 41, 65, 67, 69, 91, 109, 115, 157, 193, 197, 199, 203, 204, 205, 206, 208, 210, 213, 215, 231
Scottish Football League 13, 27, 28, 85
Scottish Junior Cup 5, 23, 65
Scottish League 23
Scottish PFA Manager of the Year 231
Scottish PFA Player of the Year 107, 123, 231
Scottish Premier League 107, 115, 155, 218
Scottish Qualifying Cup 5, 23
Scullion, Conor 219
Second Division 1, 3, 5, 11, 13, 19, 21, 25, 33, 35, 41, 50, 51, 54, 61, 63, 65, 67, 82, 83, 85, 88, 91, 96, 104, 105, 107, 109, 120, 123, 136, 137, 139, 155, 162, 188, 191, 197, 218
Shankland, Lawrence v, 201, 202, 203, 204, 205, 207, 208, 211, 212, 213, 214, 215, 217, 221, 222, 223, 224, 225, 226, 227, 228, 229, 231
Sharp, Lee 157, 181, 188
Shettleston Juniors 107
Shielfield Park, Berwick 73, 102, 124, 132, 170, 181, 187
Shyberry Excelsior Stadium, Airdrie 224, 228
Simpson, Harry 11, 15, 16, 17, 19, 29, 30, 31, 32, 33
Simpson, Jocky 46, 47, 49, 50
Skol Cup 109
Sludden, John 107, 109, 115, 119, 120, 123, 124, 126, 128, 130, 132, 133, 134, 135, 136, 233
Smith, Albert 54, 57, 58, 59, 60, 61
Smith, Angus 117
Smith, Bob 55, 56, 57, 58, 59, 60, 61
Smith, Bobby 81, 82
Smith, Callum 217
Smith, Colin 139, 177
Smith, Graeme 207
Smith, Henry 142, 144, 157, 162, 170, 174, 177, 179, 181, 184, 186, 187
Smith, Jimmy 37, 39, 40, 41, 42, 43, 44, 45, 46, 47, 48, 49, 50, 233
Smith, Kevin 204
Smith, Mike 117
Smith, Paul 142, 147, 153, 161, 166, 172, 174, 177, 179, 181, 184, 186, 187, 188
Smith, Tom 148, 151, 165, 167, 170, 177, 179, 181, 184, 186, 187, 188
Somerset Park xiii, 3, 5, 7, 9, 11, 15, 16, 17, 19, 23, 29, 30, 31, 32, 37, 44, 45, 46, 47, 48, 49, 53, 55, 56, 57, 58, 59, 60, 61, 71, 73, 75, 77, 79,

80, 81, 82, 91, 97, 99, 101, 102, 103, 104, 111, 113, 115, 117, 119, 123, 124, 126, 128, 130, 132, 134, 135, 136, 153, 155, 162, 170, 174, 177, 179, 181, 184, 186, 187, 193, 199, 203, 205, 206, 210, 218, 219, 220, 221, 222, 223, 224, 225, 226, 228, 231, 233
Somerset Road end 120, 211
Spain Park, Aberdeen 203
Stainrod, Simon 139
Stair Park, Stranraer 73, 102, 132, 159, 179, 186, 206, 221, 224
Stark's Park, Kirkcaldy 61, 103, 207, 211, 214, 219, 221, 225
Station Park, Forfar 48, 59, 77, 81, 97, 202, 213, 222, 226
Steele, Jock 56, 57
Steen, Tom 27
Stenhousemuir 39, 46, 49, 54, 57, 58, 69, 73, 82, 88, 93, 103, 104, 109, 111, 117, 123, 126, 132, 136, 146, 147, 153, 154, 157, 162, 174, 179, 184, 187, 232
Stevenson, Bobby 77, 79, 82
Stevenson, Ryan 195
Stewart, Davy, 25
Stewart, Ross 210
Stewart's Tailors 7
Stirling Albion 107, 111, 115, 119, 120, 124, 130, 135, 139, 147, 165, 218
Stirling, Ian 101, 104
Stockholm 43
Stoke City 41
Strain, David 56, 57, 58, 59, 60, 61
Stranraer 73, 79, 93, 94, 102, 104, 109, 115, 119, 124, 132, 135, 139, 142, 149, 153, 159, 177, 179, 181, 186, 198, 199, 201, 202, 203, 205, 206, 214, 215, 216, 218, 221, 223, 224, 228, 233
Summers, Eddie 54, 55, 58, 59, 60, 61, 71

T

Taggart, Scott 201
Tannadice Park, Dundee 7, 11, 16, 31, 42, 46, 59, 80
Tarrant, Neil 195
Taylor, Jock 56, 57, 58, 59, 60, 61
Taylor, Phil 139
Telfer, John 73, 75, 77, 79, 80, 81
Templeton, Henry 107, 109, 111, 115, 117, 119, 120, 123, 124, 126, 127, 128, 130, 132, 134, 135, 136
Third Lanark 42, 46, 49, 50, 88, 99, 102, 195
Thompson, Frank 51, 53, 54, 55
Thompson, Kenny 117
Thomson, Adam 97, 101, 102, 103, 104
Thomson, Bobby 69, 73, 74, 75, 79, 80, 81, 82
Thomson, Steve 165
Thomson, Jason 201
Thomson, David 15, 16, 17, 19, 25, 29, 30, 31, 32, 34
Thomson, H (1912/13) 30
Thorburn, Grant 193
Thornhill 5
Tickle, Bert 5, 9, 11, 15, 16, 17, 19, 29
Tolland, Danny 39, 40, 44, 45, 46, 47, 48, 49, 50
Torbet 54, 56, 57, 58, 59, 60, 61
Traynor x, xi, 145, 155, 158, 167, 170, 174, 176, 177, 179, 181, 184, 185, 186, 187, 188
Trouten 204, 210, 213
Turnbull 44, 45, 46, 47, 48, 49, 50
Turner, Kyle 215

U

Ure, Ian 65

V

Vale of Leven 15, 16, 23, 24, 29, 32
Vallauris 157
Vaughan, Lewis 201, 207
Volunteer Park, Armadale 49

W

Waite, David 193, 221, 222, 223
Walker, Tommy 107, 109, 113, 124, 125, 126, 128, 130, 132, 134, 135, 136
Wallace, Ryan 206
Wallace Tower 7
Wallacetown 3
Walsall 191
Walters, Jacky 44
Ward, John 115
Ward, Mark 147, 177
Warrender, Bobby 67
Watson, Craig 214
Watson, George 107, 113, 119, 124, 126, 128, 130, 132, 134, 135, 136
Watson, Gregg 56
Watson, Jock 46, 48, 49
Watson, Paul 147, 151, 177, 179, 181, 184, 186, 187
Welsh, Peter 128, 135
West Ham United 7, 25, 147
West Sound Big Match Trophy 199
White, Sprigger 18, 23, 25, 29, 30, 31, 32
Whitehead, Ian 197
Whithorn 5
Whittle, Brian 142
Wilson, Kenny 119, 120, 124, 126, 128, 130, 131, 132, 134, 135, 136
Wimbledon 142
Woodburn, John 44
Wrexham 147
Wright, Kieran 219

Y

Young, Jake 80, 82
Young, Jason 162

www.ingramcontent.com/pod-product-compliance
Lightning Source LLC
Chambersburg PA
CBHW071620170426
13195CB00038B/1584